Second Edition

Thinking Strategies for Science

Grades 5–12

*I wrote the first edition of this book before I retired from
classroom teaching and, 14 years later, I still have the same warm fuzzy
feelings about the students and their influence on me that I did then.
So I'm leaving the tribute to them intact. I know that readers will understand.*

Second Edition

Thinking Strategies for Science

Grades 5–12

Sally Berman

CORWIN PRESS
A SAGE Company
Thousand Oaks, CA 91320

Copyright © 2008 by Corwin Press

For information:

Corwin Press
A SAGE Company
2455 Teller Road
Thousand Oaks, California 91320
www.corwinpress.com

SAGE Ltd.
1 Oliver's Yard
55 City Road
London EC1Y 1SP
United Kingdom

SAGE India Pvt. Ltd.
B 1/I 1 Mohan Cooperative
   Industrial Area
Mathura Road, New Delhi
India 110 044

SAGE Asia-Pacific Pte. Ltd.
33 Pekin Street #02-01
Far East Square
Singapore 048763

Printed in the United States of America.

Library of Congress Cataloging-in-Publication Data

Berman, Sally.
Thinking strategies for science, grades 5–12/Sally Berman.—2nd ed.
   p. cm.
Rev ed. of: Catch them thinking in science. 1993.
Includes bibliographical references and index.
ISBN 978-1-4129-6288-9 (cloth)
ISBN 978-1-4129-6289-6 (pbk.)

   1. Science—Study and teaching—Handbooks, manuals, etc. I. Berman, Sally. Catch them thinking in science. II. Title.

Q181.B532 2009
507.1′2—dc22   2008006268

This book is printed on acid-free paper.

08   09   10   11   12   10 9 8 7 6 5 4 3 2 1

Acquisitions Editor:	Cathy Hernandez
Associate Editor:	Megan Bedell
Production Editor:	Cassandra Margaret Seibel
Copy Editor:	Edward Meidenbauer
Typesetter:	C&M Digitals (P) Ltd.
Proofreader:	Susan Schon
Indexer:	Jean Casalegno
Cover Designer:	Lisa Riley

Contents

Preface

CATCH YOUR STUDENTS THINKING IN SCIENCE

As classroom teachers, we know that students do not acquire thinking skills by studying content in traditional ways. We also know that much of the content that students acquire from teacher presentation followed by repetition and drill is quickly forgotten, and we know, or at least suspect, that this learning process does not promote the development of lifelong thinking and learning skills (Caine, Caine, McClintic, & Klimek, 2005). As a conscientious classroom teacher, you have probably been wondering how to design science lessons that encourage your students to become better thinkers. The organization of this book is designed to help you do just that. We science teachers proclaim that we want to help our students develop their thinking skills, but we very often try to build those skills without following a blueprint. We may get lucky. We may also leave less-gifted students feeling baffled, frustrated, and confused.

HOW IS THIS BOOK ORGANIZED?

Part I: Gathering Information

Part I of this book describes and gives some examples of activities that are useful to students who are gathering information. Useful higher-level thinking must begin here. Students cannot process what they do not have. The activities help hook student interest, facilitate their learning, and make them responsible for doing the work that you want them to do. As students do these activities, they will make their thinking visible by using grids for organizing information. They will also be asked to begin keeping a class log or journal, so they will need to have notebooks in which they can keep their logs or journals organized. You may have them use whatever type of notebook you prefer. I like three-ring binders; they allow students to insert artifacts that are related to the log or journal entries. Part I includes an activity that introduces students to think-pair-share, a powerful technique for gathering answers to questions that students may not have used before. It encourages students to become more reflective and less impulsive by asking them to wait until called on before telling you (and the rest of the class) their answers to questions. Stress the idea that by decreasing their impulsive urges to blurt out answers, students allow the whole class to gather better information.

Part II: Processing Information

Part II includes activities that can be used to process information. This is where the fun really begins! Students are asked to analyze, visualize, organize, and explain information in a variety of ways. Cooperative learning enhances this phase of their learning. Be sure that your students understand the skills that make cooperative groups function effectively and the roles that members of cooperative groups are asked to perform. You can find a thorough explanation of cooperative group skills and roles in *Blueprints for Achievement in the Cooperative Classroom* (Bellanca & Fogarty, 2001, Corwin Press). Individuals may be asked to do a rough draft of many of the assigned activities to share with teammates in class. When the teams get together, everyone benefits from the exchange of ideas.

Students will use a variety of graphic organizers to make their thinking visible as they do the activities. They will use webs, Venn diagrams, fishbones, matrices (grids), and they will be asked to take good notes (be good information gatherers) as they carry out their assigned cooperative roles. Several of the activities involve brainstorming. You may want to remind students of the DOVE guidelines (Bellanca & Fogarty, 2001) before they begin these activities. There is a DOVE guidelines reproducible master at the back of this book that makes an excellent transparency for the overhead projector or interactive whiteboard (see page 90).

Part III: Analyzing and Applying Information

Part III describes activities that can be used to analyze and apply information. Look at the products of these activities as *alternatives* to traditional assessment tools. The best products again come from cooperative learning teams. Students are asked to design products that combine verbal, visual, and analytical skills. Their visible thinking appears in mind maps, storyboards and other graphics, and right-angle thinking diagrams. This part stresses writing skills. They may complain that the activities are hard, but they will come away from them with a better understanding of the topic than you may have believed possible.

Part IV: Designing Your Own Activities

This is a new section that I am including in the second edition to address a concern voiced by readers of the first edition: "How do we and other teachers design our own activities or lessons to catch our students thinking in science?" In this chapter, you will find several clear guidelines to follow in designing lessons that develop specific thinking skills. In writing this section, I followed my own advice and became very metacognitive, reflecting on my classroom experiences and lesson-planning sessions and sharing with you what worked best for me. The pointers in this new chapter direct you to

- Use the activity model described below as a template for new lessons
- Become very metacognitive in planning, monitoring, and reflecting on these new lessons
- Tap into varied resources to find ideas for lessons
- Remember to align the activity that you are planning with national science standards and specific thinking skills

- Connect thinking skills to use of graphic organizers to help students' brains pattern new learning
- Structure and monitor cooperative learning groups carefully
- Have fun in and out of the classroom

Read through Part IV carefully. Remember to start with simple lessons and you will find yourself gaining confidence in your ability to design lessons that help your students become lifelong learners.

Each chapter in these four parts is organized into these sections. Think of this organization as providing you with a model for planning your own activities.

1. **Background** includes a brief theoretical basis and/or rationale for the activity and connects the activity to prior or future learning.

2. **Standards** aligns the activity with one or more of the national science standards.

3. **Thinking Skills** names the specific thinking micro-skills stressed in the activity.

4. **Focus Activity** describes the hook that is used to engage students in the lesson.

5. **Objectives** names the skills that the lesson is intended to develop.

6. **Input** outlines the materials that the teacher needs and the frontload that the students need to do the lesson successfully.

7. **Activity** describes what the students and teacher will actually do during the lesson.

8. **Cognitive Discussion** tells how the students and teacher will process the content that has been learned by doing the lesson.

9. **Metacognitive Discussion** suggests questions that students can use to reflect on the effectiveness of the learning process and how the process can be applied to learn new content.

10. **Closure and Assessment** provides a follow-up to the activity; it usually includes a sharing of the product of the activity; it may suggest a new, related activity; and it usually includes an activity-specific assessment.

You may be able to use some lessons exactly as they appear. Others may focus on specific content that is not included in your science curriculum. Let the latter serve as models for your own lessons that do fit your curriculum. Once you have seen examples of "The People Search," for instance, you can write your own. As you develop your lessons, let the organization of this book serve as a guide for developing your students' thinking skills.

This book's organization was inspired by Oliver Wendell Holmes, who said,

There are one-story intellects, two-story intellects, and three-story intellects with skylights. All fact-collectors, who have no aim beyond their facts, are one-story men. Two-story men compare, reason, generalize, using the labors of the fact-collectors as well as their own. Three-story men idealize, imagine, predict; their best illumination comes from above, through the skylight. (Holmes, 1916)

A WORD ABOUT PROCESSING

Looking back and reflecting cognitively and metacognitively on what has been done, what has been learned, and what aspects of the activity can be transferred to new situations is a key component of all of the activities in all three parts. Often this involves having all groups present their products, applications, or ideas for transfer to the rest of the class. This sharing is called a *wraparound*. You may have teams draw numbers to decide who presents first, who presents second, and so on during the wraparound, or you may ask the class if teams would like to volunteer to decide who answers first, who answers second, and so forth. It is important to make the order of presentation strictly random by asking for volunteers or handing out numbers. Students who perceive that you are calling on them because you believe that they are less skilled or less prepared than others and you want to teach them a lesson are unlikely to become productively involved in the activities. I find that a good preparation for metacognitive wraparounds is asking students to write in their logs, using Mrs. Potter's Questions (Bellanca & Fogarty, 2001) as the cue for the log entry. (See page 91 for a blackline master.)

Mrs. Potter's Questions ask:

What were we supposed to do?

What did we do well?

What would we do differently next time?

Do you need any help?

I like to add one more question: How can we use the strategies we learned or the information that we gained in other activities or in other settings? Individual students write the answers in their logs. Students may discuss their thoughts with their teammates or pair and share. You can then draw names out of a hat or ask for volunteers to share their ideas with the rest of the class. The more you share information and ideas, the more valuable the lessons become. I encourage students to be aware of their use of the information or strategies in other classrooms or in everyday life.

One word of caution: It takes time to do thinking skill activities and to monitor the use of these skills in the classroom. You must decide whether you want to take the time to do a good job, or whether short-term memorization and high scores on multiple choice tests satisfy you. Please consider, as you make your decision, that factual knowledge in science doubles every year. By the time your students finish their formal education and become independent adults, many of your facts will be outdated. Memorizers may be left behind. Thinkers will not be.

The strategies and activities that I have included in this book are ones that I found very effective with my students. I used all of them in my classroom at one time or another. Do not let the variety overwhelm you. Pick one or two from each part to try, and then add others as you become more familiar with the first few. Get other teachers involved in using the strategies. Form a support team so that you can help each other. Fine tune your lessons as you try them, and celebrate success when it happens. Include your students in your celebrations. Catch them being good at thinking in science!

WHAT'S NEW IN THE SECOND EDITION

The Standards

I wrote the first edition of this book in 1993, before the publication of the National Science Standards. Since their publication in 1995, I've wanted to do a second edition in which each activity is aligned with one or more of the standards. Because the focus of this book is on developing *thinking skills* in science, I've focused on the Unifying Concepts and Processes and Science as Inquiry standards. Individual teachers can align the activities with grade level or content area standards as desired.

Teaching Thinking Skills

I've added sections addressing the importance of teaching thinking skills and some of the myriad ways in which thinking skills can be taught. I believe that these sections serve two purposes: They introduce you to some of the research that addresses the importance of teaching thinking and they serve to emphasize the primary purpose of this book which is to focus on helping students to become better thinkers and self-directed learners.

Reaching Students With Special Needs and English Language Learners

There are new sections in which I've discussed ways in which the requirements of English language learners and students with special needs can be addressed. I know that the ideas I've included are far from all-inclusive, but they do provide some helpful guidelines and will give you some ideas about where to find more help.

Assessments

For each activity, I've included assessment suggestions. I do not want you to think that these are replacements for the learning log that is emphasized throughout the book. I mean these to be tasks that can be done in addition to the log.

A Quick Look at Science Inquiry

Some readers of the first edition felt that more activities using *inquiry* needed to be included in the book. This section, located in the Introduction, includes an overview of three models of inquiry-based learning and an explanation of how this book supports the inquiry model.

"Do It Yourself"

In the final chapter of this book, you will find guidelines for developing your own activities. Please remember that simplicity is the key when you begin to develop lessons of your own. Many of the lessons in this book are simple in design, and they are very effective in helping students to develop more effective thinking skills. Also remember to have fun with lesson design. As Sylwester (1995) says, "Emotion drives attention which drives learning." Making learning fun makes it more permanent.

The Three-Story Intellect

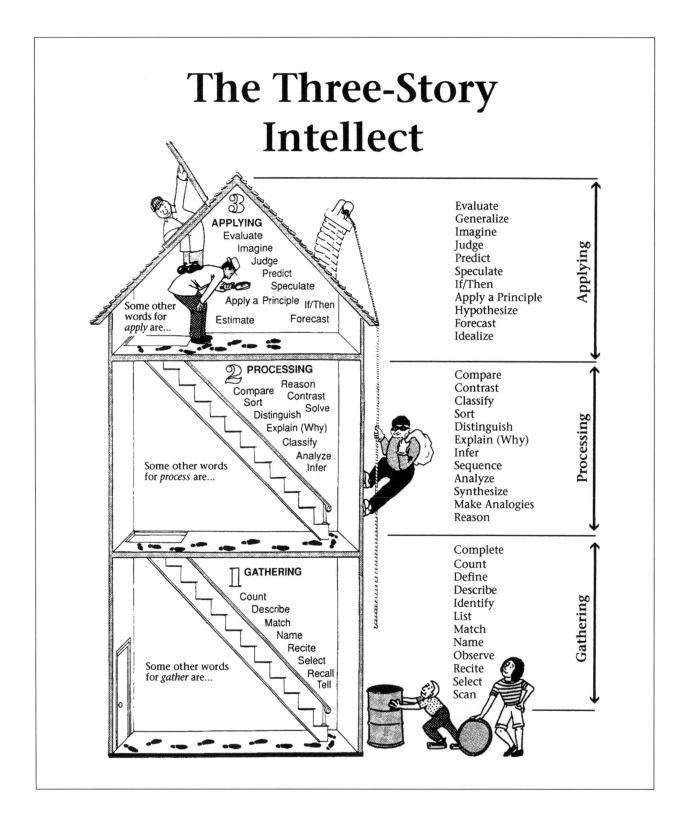

③ APPLYING

Evaluate
Imagine
Judge
Predict
Speculate
Apply a Principle   If/Then
Estimate   Forecast

Some other words for *apply* are...

② PROCESSING

Reason
Compare   Contrast
Sort   Solve
Distinguish
Explain (Why)
Classify
Analyze
Infer

Some other words for *process* are...

① GATHERING

Count
Describe
Match
Name
Recite
Select
Recall
Tell

Some other words for *gather* are...

Applying

Evaluate
Generalize
Imagine
Judge
Predict
Speculate
If/Then
Apply a Principle
Hypothesize
Forecast
Idealize

Processing

Compare
Contrast
Classify
Sort
Distinguish
Explain (Why)
Infer
Sequence
Analyze
Synthesize
Make Analogies
Reason

Gathering

Complete
Count
Define
Describe
Identify
List
Match
Name
Observe
Recite
Select
Scan

Acknowledgments

The whole thing started because of the kids—those wonderful, amazing, frustrating, challenging, warm, exciting students with whom I work 185 days every year. I needed to know that we were speaking the same language and that they were puzzling out answers to problems and making connections with prior content knowledge in science and with life outside of the science classroom. I wanted to focus their efforts on developing teamwork and thoughtfulness. I looked around for materials that contained cooperative and cognitive activities in science. None existed. I needed to invent my own student-centered lessons or go back to doing things the teacher-centered way. The latter was unthinkable. The students deserved better. The students of Palatine High School provided the primary motivation for writing this book.

It must have been serendipity. When I was about one-fourth of the way through the project, I mentioned to Jim Bellanca and Robin Fogarty that I was writing a book of activities for students to use in my classroom. Jim said, "Bring it to us—we'll publish it." Robin said, "We're really looking for a *Catch Them Thinking in Science*. Will you write it for us?" What began as a very chemistry-specific work evolved into a book that included sample lessons in all science disciplines. Robin's question gave me the courage to step outside of my specific content area and expand my horizons, and Jim and Robin's encouragement kept me going.

Fellow Palatine High School science teachers Ed Richardson, Floyd Rogers, Kathy Seilheimer, Sue Anderson, and Tony Krotz loaned me biology, earth science, and physical science books that provided content ideas for some of the lessons. Gary Kraft's need to teach his students to organize information in Venn diagrams led to the frontload activity for "Frogs and Salamanders." Roy Schodtler served as sounding board and devil's advocate. His valuable questions guided the revision of several lessons. Jim Tefft took the time to explain some basic physics to me until I could not help but understand it—which is quite an accomplishment. Ken Spengler, department chairman, mentor, good friend, and chemistry buddy, has given me ideas and inspiration for as long as we have taught together—which is almost 30 years. He developed the prototype of the "Letter to Uncle Chester" from a suggestion that we heard at a Chemistry West meeting. Bob Zuidema, a Palatine High School physics teacher of almost fifteen years ago, planted the seeds for "Hide in Plain Sight" before he left us. Those seeds may have taken a long time to germinate, but they popped up right when I needed them most. Mike Offutt of Barrington High School confirmed my belief in storyboarding. Mike's students draw comic strips, which are very much the same thing. Buddy Hughes, commercial artist and former Palatine High School student and baseball pitcher, actually introduced me to storyboarding as it is used in advertising in the late 1970s. I did not see the use then, but storyboards have become one of my favorite cooperative, cognitive activities. Lee Marek, DeWayne Lieneman, Bob Lewis, and other Chemistry West regulars have encouraged the humorous twist found in some of the lessons in this book. I can never thank them enough for sharing so many of their own lessons and ideas over the years. Some strategies, like the black boxes in "Mental Modeling," have been around for so long, in so many different forms, that I do not really know where or when they were first invented—and I cannot find anyone else who knows either.

My husband, Al, endured being a writing widower nights, weekends, and during our vacations from school. He found ways to keep himself amused while I typed (or sat and stared at the wall asking myself, "Where am I going with this one?"). He was and is my rock, my best friend, my champion, my knight in shining armor. He brought me coffee, aspirin, and love, took messages, ran errands, absorbed my frustrations, picked up Chinese food, bought groceries, encouraged me when the going got rough, proofread copy, bought me flowers, and kept me believing that I could finish this project.

Thank you everyone who helped and encouraged me, and thank you, kids. This book would not have been imagined had it not been for you.

Thank you also to my new professional friends at Corwin Press. Megan Bedell digested the peer reviews and developed a list of key revision points that focused my work. As we entered the editing and production phases needed to get the book into print, Megan massaged and tweaked the initial draft to smooth out the rough spots, and she asked for clarification or additional information as needed to make the book more reader friendly. I've always said that an excellent editor is a critical element in the development of a good book, and the editor gets very little of the credit for the finished product. I want every reader to know just how important Megan's guidance has been in the writing of this second edition.

A good production editor gives a book its polished appearance and enhances its overall reader appeal. I thank Cassandra Seibel for her hard work and attention to detail that gave this book its structure and professional look.

Careful copy editing clarifies meaning, eliminates redundancies, smoothes transitions, and enhances a manuscript in many other ways. My thanks go to Edward Meidenbauer for his thoughtful, careful work that strengthened this book. Edward's light hand retained my voice while strengthening the book.

PUBLISHER'S ACKNOWLEDGMENTS

Corwin Press gratefully acknowledges the contributions of the following reviewers:

William C. Anderson, AP Biology Teacher
Unionville High School, Kennett Square, PA

Nancy T. Davis, Associate Professor of Middle and Secondary Education
Florida State University, Tallahassee, FL

Jean Eames, Biology and Chemistry Teacher
Benson Polytechnic High School, Portland, OR

Ken Garwick, Sixth Grade Teacher
Marlatt Elementary School, Manhattan, KS

David L. Haury, Associate Professor of Science Education
Ohio State University, Columbus, OH

Emily Lin, Assistant Professor of Teacher Education
University of Nevada, Las Vegas

Leah Melber, Assistant Professor of Curriculum and Instruction
California State University, Los Angeles

About the Author

 **Sally Berman** is an experienced, creative facilitator of interactive workshops during which educators learn how to create classrooms in which their students develop teamwork, cognition, metacognition, and self-evaluation skills. Sally developed and tested many of her ideas during her 30 years of science teaching at a large high school in the Chicago suburbs.

Sally received her AB in Chemistry and Mathematics in 1964 and her MS in Chemical Education in 1969. In the mid-1980s, feeling a need for professional rejuvenation, she embarked on a learning quest that led to work with a number of outstanding educators and theorists. A few of these were Jim Bellanca, David and Roger Johnson, David Lazear, Kay Burke, and Robin Fogarty.

Using her newly acquired information, Sally created and led workshops and graduate courses for a variety of clients. She has worked with educators and industrial trainers from the United States, Canada, the Netherlands, Britain, Eastern Europe, and Australia.

Sally lives with Al, her best friend and husband of 37 years, near Ontonagon, Michigan, on the south shore of Lake Superior. They met when both were teaching at Palatine High School in Palatine, Illinois. Sally says, "It was love in the lounge!" Sally taught chemistry, and Al taught English and coached wrestling. Sally does not get up in the dark; she does, on occasion, stay up until dawn. She is sometimes compared with the Kay Thompson creation, Eloise.

Introduction

WHY TEACH THINKING SKILLS?

We know that students who possess good thinking skills develop deeper understandings within and across content disciplines and become self-regulated learners (Cognitive Skills Group, 1998). Self-regulated learners take charge of their own learning processes by monitoring the effectiveness of their learning strategies, adjusting learning behaviors that do not seem to be producing desired results, and transferring their learning to new situations (Caine, Caine, McClintic, & Klimek, 2005). In 1991, the SCANS Report emphasized the importance of developing lifelong learning and transfer skills (SCANS, 1991). The United States Department of Labor formed SCANS, the Secretary's Commission on Achieving Necessary Skills, to determine the competencies that workers would need to be successful in the 21st century workplace. The commission identified five competencies:

- Resources of time, money, materials, and skills
- Interpersonal abilities of teamwork, leadership, and respect for diversity
- Information acquisition, organization, interpretation, and transfer
- Systems understanding, monitoring, design, and improvement
- Technology selection, use, application, and troubleshooting

In a 2003 follow-up to the SCANS report, the METIRI group, a company that offers a broad range of consulting services focusing on effective teaching and learning, concluded that globalization and the Internet require individuals to be self-directed learners who can analyze new conditions as they arise, identify, and learn the new skills that dealing with these conditions will require, and independently find a way to deal with the challenges (METIRI Group, 2003). We do students a great disservice if we persist in using traditional "sit and git" instruction.

HOW TO TEACH THINKING SKILLS

So now you may be wondering how to teach students the thinking skills that they need to become self-regulated learners. Weiss (1993) suggests that students need to see that improved thinking skills lead to increased content learning. If students learn how to identify the most important points in a reading selection, for example, they will become more effective at learning by reading. Using graphic organizers appropriately will help students become more strategic learners, encourage them to process information at more complex levels, and by reducing the demands for semantic information processing, help students with learning disabilities develop deep understanding of content (Ellis, 2004).

One powerful technique that you can use is to model your own thinking processes. As you explain how to solve a problem, describe your thinking out loud. As you give instructions for a hands-on activity, stop to explain why you think the procedure will work. Ask yourself, out loud, "What if this doesn't work?" or "What do I want to learn by doing this?" or "What might be a different way to do this?" Once students have heard your internal dialogue, give them a problem to solve or an issue to discuss and assign roles: one student is to be the Thinker and the other is to be the Prober. The Thinker works through the problem, talking about what he or she is doing, and the Prober asks questions such as "Can you explain what you did there?" or "Why did you decide to take that step?" or "Tell me more about your thinking." This kind of paired thinking helps students become more metacognitive in monitoring the effectiveness of their thinking and their actions.

Many of the activities in this book use graphic organizers that make information more precise, structure the information in useful ways, enhance learning for a wide range of students, and encourage the development of both critical and creative thinking skills and communication skills (Ellis, 2004). Other activities ask students to make careful observations, describe what and how they observed, and ask questions about information that has been presented to them in a variety of ways. As students participate in these activities, they come to a deeper understanding of the content and skills that they are learning while embedding that learning more firmly in their memories (Caine et al., 2005).

What About Students With Special Needs?

Research shows that students with special needs experience success in developing thinking skills when they engage in lessons that explicitly mediate the skills and bridge their use to everyday life examples (Galyam & LeGrange, 2003). Feuerstein (1980) describes mediation as a process by which a more knowledgeable person prompts a less knowledgeable person to label, compare, categorize, and give meaning to a present experience as it relates to prior and future ones. His model of mediated learning incorporates four elements:

- *reciprocity,* which establishes a safe-risk connection of acceptance and trust;
- *intent,* which focuses attention on the task at hand;
- *meaning,* which connects the learning to prior knowledge and places it in the context of appropriate patterns of information; and
- *transcendence,* which expands learning into everyday life and promotes transfer (Greenberg, 1996).

In a typical classroom, one teacher would be hard pressed to offer mediated learning experiences to all of the students all of the time, and that is where cooperative learning groups become one of the teacher's most valuable tools.

Here is how cooperative learning aligns with Feuerstein's mediated learning model.

Reciprocity: When cooperative learning is used skillfully, students learn to trust their teammates. They share responsibility for group leadership, functioning, and completion of an assigned task, and they practice use of social skills like giving encouragement, questioning ideas, contributing a fair share, and taking turns.

Intent: Cooperative group learning involves the completion of an assigned task. Within each group, students perform assigned roles, and each student knows that he or she is expected to contribute to the final group product. The teacher monitors groups as they work and intervenes to correct misunderstandings of content information or instructions. The teacher will often give groups a detailed checklist or rubric that they use to evaluate their progress toward completing the task. Each member of a group knows that he or she may be questioned about the content learning or the process the group is using to complete the task.

Meaning: As teammates work toward completion of the task, the teacher listens to group discussions to check on the accuracy and completeness of content learning. The teacher intervenes if a group has an incorrect understanding of content or skill learning. If a majority of the groups in the class seem to have difficulty with some of the content information, the teacher will take time for whole-class direct instruction followed by group clarification and processing.

Transcendence: At the end of a group activity, individuals process and reflect on their learning and brainstorm ways in which they can transfer their knowledge and skills to new settings. Members of a team share these individual reflections and transfer applications, and the teacher will often lead a whole-class processing session.

Cooperative learning groups become in-class resource groups for special needs students, and their teammates benefit from the cooperative activities by learning leadership and communication skills and, because teaching reveals incomplete or inaccurate knowledge by uncovering misunderstandings, teammates of special needs students improve and deepen their own learning. And as Kluger (2007) reports in his article on how birth order shapes our destinies, the mentoring that students provide to each other in cooperative learning groups can actually raise their scores on IQ tests.

What About English Language Learners?

English language learners benefit from mediated learning and other classroom practices that scaffold their transition as they learn to think in a new language. Students who speak English as a first language often have difficulty keeping up with a fast-paced oral activity, like brainstorming, when no time is given to collect their thoughts. For English speakers and English language learners alike, strategies such as using wait time or think-pair-share slow down the action and provide an opportunity for students to process more deeply and generate a wider variety of ideas. Teachers need to consider what Meyer (2000) calls the "learning load" of a classroom activity and make adaptations that scaffold learning. Tools for organizing thinking that rely on semantic processing help English language learners connect language to content (Beckett & Haley, 2000), and this book features several such tools, including K-W-L, the reading prediction guide, and mind mapping.

The American Federation of Teachers (2002) states that a safe and orderly learning environment is perhaps the most important feature of a classroom in which

English language learners can thrive. Carefully structured cooperative learning activities provide English language learners a safe-risk climate in which to practice and develop fluency in their new language and develop confidence in their language skills (Boothe, 2000). These activities give English as a second language (ESL) students an opportunity to not only speak the language but to hear it spoken by teachers and peers who are competent in their use of English (Brilliant, 2001). ESL teachers have commented to me that cooperative learning teams give their students built-in resource groups that focus on science content learning, and that resource is invaluable to the ESL students as they work to master both the language and the science learning.

HOW TO ASSESS YOUR STUDENTS

One method of assessment, the log, is used throughout this book. Other activity-specific assessment tools are suggested at the end of each activity.

What Is the Log?

It is a record of a student's thoughts and learnings for your class. The log includes focus writing, "Think!" (from think-pair-share), items from cognitive and metacognitive processing, sketches, spontaneous entries, and maybe some class notes.

I asked my students to begin every class session by "logging in," focusing on the prompt: "During our last class meeting, we *did what? Investigated what content? Learned what?*" I told them that the reason for this logging in was to help them connect the new lesson to prior learning, to build on what we had done during our previous class meeting. I also asked them to record unanswered questions they had about the prior learning, and I addressed these concerns for a few minutes before moving into the new lesson.

At the end of each class session, I asked students to "log out" by focusing on the prompt: "Today in class we *did what? Investigated what content? Learned what?* Here is how today's class connects to a part of my life outside of this classroom." I wanted to encourage transfer, and by asking students to make some explicit connection to another class or the everyday world as they logged out, I believe I did facilitate this ability.

Why Ask Students to Keep a Log?

A log helps students keep track of much more than new content learning. At the beginning of a new topic, students may focus by writing down their impressions or thoughts about a key word (i.e., what do they think when they hear *element, gene, ocean*).

As study of the topic proceeds, students are encouraged to jot down clarifications, corrections, and additions to their original impressions or thoughts. The log becomes a record of the progress they have made as they study the topic. At this point, it may include class notes, sketches, diagrams, lists of ideas from "Share" (think-pair-share), or personal goals for making progress in their understanding of the topic. They may write questions that they want to have answered. Encourage them to make their logs a record of their complete experience as they study the topic.

To that end, many of the cognitive and metacognitive discussions that are suggested for activities in this book involve writing or sketching log entries. As students write or draw, they clarify their thinking about the lesson. This helps them remember it better. End of class logging also provides for a quiet time for students to unwind and prepare for the next class or activity.

What Do You Do While They Log?

You log! Model the behavior that you want from them. They will perceive it as being worthwhile if they see you doing it too. The fastest way for you to discourage students' belief in logging is to neglect doing it yourself. I still have my daily log from my last year of teaching, and I treasure it. It gives me a picture of my daily activity and my ongoing metacognitive assessment of myself as a teacher.

What Are the Benefits of Logging?

Students are more focused at the beginning of class. Because you ask them to summarize the previous lesson on the topic, they find it easier to connect information. They have a running record of the development of a topic, which is invaluable when time comes to review.

Students also have fun with their logs. Many of my students recorded personal feelings and thoughts that they found very amusing a few months later. The log can become a diary as well as a record of class work and tool for reflection and improved thinking; it is important that students remember that the log is first and foremost a tool for enhancing their learning and thinking.

Is it Hard to Assess Student Logs?

Not really. Keep in mind that what you are looking for is an indication of clear expression, improved understanding, improved use of thinking skills, and honest reflection. You will soon find that you enjoy assessing logs much more than Scantron tests. They give you the opportunity to witness students' growth and progress from their perspective.

When I was teaching, I worked with five classes a day that each included 25–30 students. A sign on a junkyard helped me find a way to assess that huge number of student logs. The sign read, "GUARD DOG ON DUTY, 3 NITES PER WEEK, U PICK WHICH NITES." I read that sign and I said to myself, "Aha! I can check three log entries per grading period in detail. I do not need to read all 45 log entries for all 130 students. The students don't know that I'm not going to read every entry. I'm the guard dog AND I pick the nights!"

I told the students what I would be doing, and I asked them, "Does that mean you only want to do three complete log entries for each grading period?" They answered that they would still need to do the daily log because they did not know in advance which entries I would decide to read.

Performance-Based Assessments

Specific assessments are suggested for individual activities. Often these are extension performances that give you an opportunity to gather information about your students' use of the targeted thinking skills.

A QUICK LOOK AT SCIENCE INQUIRY

And now you may be wondering how this book aligns with the inquiry-based model of science instruction. Before I answer that question, here's a quick summary of the inquiry-based model.

In inquiry-based lessons, students gather information, question their findings, and investigate phenomena. An inquiry-based activity will include elements that are used in effective scientific investigation. In practice, inquiry-based learning and teaching usually occur along a continuum (Northwest Regional Educational Laboratory, 2007). The different levels of inquiry-based activities represent different degrees of student autonomy; at one end of the spectrum is *structured inquiry* in which students gather information and form conclusions in hands-on activities that are developed by the teacher. The students follow precise instructions, and the teacher leads small groups or the whole class in discussions in which students share conclusions and insights.

The middle ground is represented by *guided inquiry* in which students develop a procedure for investigating a problem or question that the teacher selects. The teacher monitors groups as they plan their investigations and intervenes to keep them on a productive path, and he or she leads small groups or the whole class in an end of activity idea-sharing discussion.

The greatest student autonomy is found in *student-initiated inquiry.* Here students generate an ill-structured question or problem related to a topic that the teacher chooses. Students engage in all aspects of inquiry from developing the question to be answered, to detailing the procedure for an investigation, to collecting and analyzing information, to drawing and sharing conclusions. Students need highly developed critical and creative thinking skills to participate in inquiry at this level.

Each level of inquiry-based learning requires students to possess certain basic cognitive skills. Thinking processes that are integral to scientific inquiry are: observing, classifying, inferring, deducing, making analogies, extrapolating, interpolating, synthesizing, evaluating, and imagining or intuiting (Hassard, 2004). Often, students have not developed these skills because their learning has been a product of the direct-instruction lesson model. This book is designed to help you nurture your students' development of inquiry-based thinking skills. Many of the activities fall into the structured or guided inquiry parts of the spectrum. As you browse through the activities, make special note of the targeted thinking skills and ask yourself why each skill is useful to scientific investigation. Then you'll understand why I believe that as students work in your classroom, it is vital that you *catch them thinking*.

PART I

Gathering Information

1

The People Search

Getting to Know You

BACKGROUND

As students participate in a People Search, they recall prior knowledge, explain or teach information to their classmates, listen to one another for understanding, use the vocabulary of the unit that they are about to study, and interact with one another, exchanging answers in a safe-risk climate.

STANDARDS

The activity aligns with Science as Inquiry Standard 1: abilities necessary to do scientific inquiry. As students seek People Search answers, they conduct mini-interviews, and interviewing is an important information gathering tool. As students answer questions, they are practicing explaining and other communication skills.

THINKING SKILLS

Recalling, Describing, Identifying, Reciting

FOCUS ACTIVITY

Give or review the rules for doing a People Search. Students are to get out of their desks and move around the room. They approach a classmate, use good eye contact, and use the classmate's name as they ask, "Can you give me an answer?" They may say, "I can answer number 3 for you. Would you be able to answer a different question for me?" Remind students that when they sign each others' People Search sheets, they signify their ability to answer whatever item they have signed their names to. As they give and receive signatures, they learn the answers to the items on the People Search. They must obtain the signature of a different classmate for each item on the People Search. Set a time limit; one minute per item is a starting point. You can always extend the time limit as needed.

OBJECTIVES

To transfer prior knowledge to the new unit of study and to communicate that knowledge to one's classmates; to begin using the vocabulary of the new unit of study and to obtain a glimpse of the content of the unit.

INPUT

Explain to the students how important it is to express themselves clearly and to check for understanding by having the student for whom they are signing repeat or paraphrase the answer. Encourage students to take notes on their People Search sheets about answers that they may forget. Remind students that their signatures mean they have the answers to the items for which they sign and that they may be called on to give those answers during a class discussion which will follow the People Search.

ACTIVITY

1. Distribute a copy of the People Search to each student. (Two different People Searches are provided on pages 5 and 6. Feel free to use the reproducible master on page 92 to create your own People Search.) Ask a student to review the instructions for doing the activity.

2. Signal when time is up and ask all students to please return to their seats.

COGNITIVE DISCUSSION

Go over the People Search item by item. Encourage students to take notes during the discussion. Call on students at random to give the answers. Below is one effective strategy for calling on students.

Call on a student, selected at random, and ask that student who signed his or her sheet for Item 1. Then ask the student who signed the sheet to give the answer. If the answer is incomplete or incorrect, ask for volunteers to add to the answer. Then call on a different student and ask that student who signed his or her sheet for Item 2. Again, the student who signed is asked to give the answer, and the class is asked to add to the answer if necessary. The teacher may also add to the answer if he or she wishes to clarify the answer or introduce additional information. The random questioning and answering continue until the last item on the People Search is answered.

Another effective strategy is to call on a student, selected at random, and ask that student who signed his or her sheet. Then tell the student, "Explain or tell us his or her answer in your own words." Have volunteers add to the answer if it is incomplete or incorrect. Either strategy holds students accountable for signing only if they know or can explain the answer for an item on the People Search.

METACOGNITIVE DISCUSSION

Tell the students to

1. Write down at least two new things that they learned by doing the People Search.

2. Explain why some cute items are included. A cute earth science item might be: Name three things that can rock.

3. Divide students into groups of three and have them make a list of all the new things learned from members of the group. Have them make a second list of reasons for inclusion of the cute people search items.

4. Have students outline or map (see Chapter 20) what they did well during the People Search, what they want to improve, and how the People Search helped them focus on science content learning.

CLOSURE AND ASSESSMENT

Closure: Using a medium that all students can see such as a large sheet of chart paper, an interactive whiteboard, or the blackboard, draw a web of the new learnings. To create the web, write the central idea, "New Learnings about [the topic]" in a circle in the center of a large, blank area. If you need help starting this, there is a reproducible master for a web at the end of this book (see page 100). As each group in turn tells one new thing learned by a member of the group, draw a line, like a wheel spoke, connecting the central idea to another circle in which you write the new idea. Each new idea creates a new spoke or branch in the web. Continue until the web includes all new learnings. Conclude by asking students to write a log entry that focuses on two new things they learned about the content and how they can use those things outside of class.

Assessment: Have students keep a reference list that identifies where they encounter information about the People Search items in reading assignments, hands-on activities, videos, or other class activities. Suggest that they use a matrix (see Chapter 13) to organize their information. The matrix needs to include

- the number of the People Search item,
- the date they encountered the information,
- the class activity or reading assignment, and
- the information they found.

At the end of the unit of study, tell each student to give you a copy of this reference list.

People Search: The Ground We Walk On

Directions: Find someone who can give you an answer for each of the items below. A classmate may sign for only one item, so you will need 11 different signatures. Sign only if you know the answer, or be prepared to accept the consequences!

My signature means that I . . .

1. can identify the four most common elements in the earth's crust.

   _____

2. can predict where I would go in the United States to find an active volcano.

   _____

3. can describe the appearance of marble.

   _____

4. do not take good grades for granite!

   _____

5. can guess why a compass goes crazy in northeast Minnesota.

   _____

6. like rocking chairs.

   _____

7. can name three kinds of rock.

   _____

8. have used lava soap.

   _____

9. can explain what limestone and coal have in common.

   _____

10. can compare the properties of quartz and diamond.

    _____

11. am using a metamorphic rock to sign this paper.

    _____

People Search: Mirror, Mirror on the Wall . . .

Directions: Find someone who can give you an answer for each of the items below. A classmate may sign for only one item, so you will need ten different signatures. Sign only if you know the answer, or be prepared to accept the consequences!

My signature means that . . .

1. I can name the process that produces an image when I look in a mirror.

   _____

2. I can explain what is wrong with a mirror image.

   _____

3. I can color inside the lines.

   _____

4. I can describe why glass makes a good mirror and brick does not.

   _____

5. I can define concave and convex.

   _____

6. I like optical illusions.

   _____

7. I can tell you what is different about reflections seen inside a spoon.

   _____

8. I can explain why roses are red and violets are blue.

   _____

9. I used a mirror this morning.

   _____

10. I can complete the quotation used as the title of this activity.

   _____

2

KNL

*What Do We **K**now?*

*What Do We **N**eed to know?*

*What Have We **L**earned?*

BACKGROUND

You may have seen this activity before. It is based on Donna Ogle's (1986) K-W-L, which she developed to help students become more active readers. I have changed "Want to know" to "Need to know" because my students answered the latter more responsibly. This is an activity that gets students hooked into a topic before formal discussion begins. It can also save you time. If they already have a lot of information about some aspects of the topic, you do not have to spend class time dispensing that information!

STANDARDS

The activity aligns with Science as Inquiry Standard 1: abilities necessary to do scientific inquiry. Students gather information by recalling prior knowledge, and they sharpen their question-asking abilities. They analyze information to fill in the "L" column and to correct any items in the "K" column that are incorrect, and they communicate their learning in the form of a final outline, map (see Chapter 20), or web (see Chapter 1).

THINKING SKILLS

Recalling, Identifying, Listing, Describing

FOCUS ACTIVITY

Set up a KNL grid on the blackboard, overhead, interactive whiteboard, or flip chart paper. There is a blackline master of the KNL grid on page 93. Using flip-chart paper to record the grid makes it possible to save it for future use. Explain to the students that they will make their contributions to the "K" and "N" columns right away and that they will fill in the "L" column toward the end of the unit.

K (What do we Know?)	N (What do we Need to know?)	L (What have we Learned?)

OBJECTIVES

To recall prior knowledge about a topic; to use that information to predict what additional information may be needed for better understanding of the topic; to begin investigation of a topic.

INPUT

See focus activity.

ACTIVITY

Divide students into groups of three. Give the groups some time to list their Ks and Ns. Be sure that each group has a recorder who writes down the list as the group brainstorms.

Call on groups for their Ks first. Ask each group for one item before any group contributes a second item. Keep going until all of the Ks for the class are recorded on the master grid (on chart paper, the overhead, the blackboard, or interactive whiteboard). Respond to contributions by saying "thank you" or by repeating the contribution as you record it. This is not the time to judge contributions. You may correct misunderstandings as you study the material.

Repeat the process for Ns.

COGNITIVE DISCUSSION

At some future time—as you complete the unit—repeat the process for Ls. This is the time to go back to the original Ks and revise any that are incorrect. Ask students to help you find them.

METACOGNITIVE DISCUSSION

Doing the sections of the grid will involve students in cognitive discussion of the material in their small groups and with the whole class. Ask them to process metacognitively by having them record new learnings and corrections of misconceptions in their logs. Have them complete logging stems like the following:

I could have used the KNL process when . . .

I will be able to use the KNL process when . . .

I am still confused about . . .

CLOSURE AND ASSESSMENT

Ask students to combine the corrected Ks and the Ls into a master list of information about the topic. Tell them that they may organize the information as an outline, map (see Chapter 20), web (see Chapter 1), or in other ways that will make it useful to them. Tell them to integrate the two lists rather than simply tacking the Ls after the corrected Ks. Have the small groups of students present their work to the class as a review of the topic.

Collect and review each student's organized information. Score the work for completeness and for organization using a rubric. You can create your own rubric at http://rubistar.4teachers.org/index.php

3

Asking Questions

What I Really Do Not Understand Is . . .

BACKGROUND

The progress of science depends on the quality and quantity of questions that scientists working in real-life laboratories ask. Students need to be taught that some questions are minnow questions (also known as skinny questions)—questions that ask for quick recall of facts and can be answered quickly. Other questions are whale questions (also known as fat questions)—questions that ask for analysis or explanation of facts or that ask for predictions based on prior knowledge. Students need to realize that the kinds of questions that they ask determine the answers they will get and that asking the right questions will help them in many different situations.

STANDARDS

This activity aligns with Science as Inquiry Standard 1: abilities necessary to do scientific inquiry and Science as Inquiry Standard 2: understandings about scientific inquiry. As students do the activity, they learn to ask questions that tap into all three stories of the Three Story Intellect. As they compare answers to the questions, they practice explaining and analyzing information and they sharpen communication skills.

THINKING SKILLS

Investigating, Identifying, Listing, Describing, Naming

FOCUS ACTIVITY

To demonstrate the difference between minnow questions and whale questions, ask the students: What natural disaster devastated the city of New Orleans in 2005?

One of them will know the right answer: Hurricane Katrina.

Then ask them: Predict the changes that might have occurred in the life of your family if you had been living in New Orleans in late August of 2005.

Stress the idea that answering a whale question completely involves asking yourself a lot of follow-up minnow questions. Give some examples—what might have happened to the electricity? Telephone service? Fuel deliveries? Ground, air, or ocean transportation? Food delivery? Availability of housing? The list goes on and on.

OBJECTIVES

To identify questions as whale questions or minnow questions; to write questions about a science topic after watching a content-related video or completing a reading assignment.

INPUT

Give students a reading assignment and time to complete it or show a content-related video. Suggest that they take notes about important information or questions that they have that are not answered by the reading or video.

Give students the Minnows and Whales graphic and the Asking Questions graphic (see pages 13 and 14).

ACTIVITY

1. Tell students to individually write at least five questions about the reading or the video. Suggest that reviewing the notes that they made can help them ask appropriate questions. Tell students that at least two of their questions must be whale questions. (Writing the individual questions may be assigned as homework.)

2. Divide students into groups of three. Have each group make a list of all the different questions asked by members of the group. Tell students to write rough drafts of their answers to the questions. Say that they will be discussing these answers with their teammates tomorrow.

3. The next day, tell students to discuss their answers with their teammates, write consensus answers, and decide which questions were whales and which were minnows. Have each group make at least two copies of its questions and consensus answers.

4. Have each group pass one copy of its questions and answers to another group.

5. Tell the groups of students to review the questions and answers from the list that they received and compare the other group's work with their own. Give the groups five to ten minutes to make the comparisons. Tell groups to record the comparisons of their work and the work from the other group. Suggest that they look for similarities and differences among the original questions, and ask them to identify instances in which different questions elicited similar answers.

6. When time is up, ask the groups to pass the other group's questions and answers back. Tell groups to examine and discuss the similarities and differences in the two sets of answers.

COGNITIVE DISCUSSION

On the blackboard, overhead projector, chart paper or interactive whiteboard, write a list of all the different questions asked by groups in the class. Call on groups in turn to contribute one question to the list. Continue until all questions are listed.

Encourage students to copy this list of questions.

Classify the questions as whale or minnow. Call on groups in turn to classify one question on the list. Continue until all questions are classified.

METACOGNITIVE DISCUSSION

Ask students to write a log entry that answers these questions:

- Which questions do you find it easier to think of?
- Why do you think that's the case?
- How might you become better at asking a variety of questions?

Call on individual students for answers to the questions.

CLOSURE AND ASSESSMENT

Closure: Tell individuals to write log entries in which they explain the differences between whale and minnow questions and the importance of each type of question.

Assessment: At the end of the next unit of study, have each student write five questions for a People Search review. Tell students that at least two of their questions must be whale questions, and require students to provide answers to their questions. Collect and score the individual student's lists of questions.

Minnows and Whales

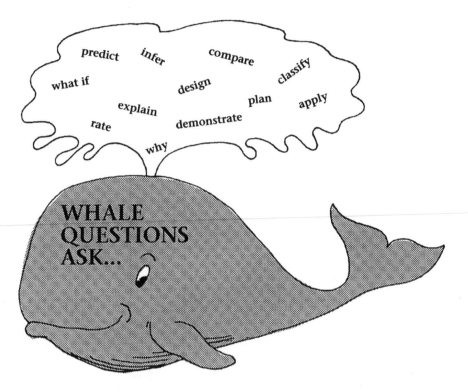

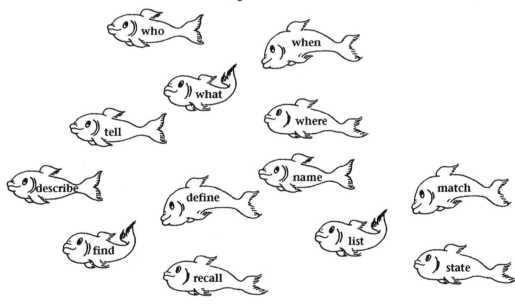

Asking Questions to Learn What I Want to Learn

Question Level	My Goal Is . . .	Some Key Words to Use Are . . .
Gathering Knowledge (First-Story Intellect)	to learn simple facts; to collect basic information	who, what, when, where, which, name, list, identify, define, how much, how many, measure, describe
Processing Knowledge (Second-Story Intellect)	to solve problems; to use knowledge in a different context or situation	compare, contrast, explain, solve, what else, instead (of), in addition to, why, my reasons are, next, in review, in conclusion, in summary, this means
Applying Knowledge (Third-Story Intellect)	to explain my opinions; to take a position; to justify an answer; to express new ideas	devise, design, develop, I predict, I believe, in my judgment, it is my opinion (that), it seems, what if

4

The Prediction Guide

Becoming More Focused Readers

BACKGROUND

Reading teachers tell us that students seldom read assigned science material because they find that they do not comprehend what they are reading or cannot decide what their teachers want them to learn by doing the reading. The prediction guide focuses their attention on the information that they are to learn from reading the text, and it also serves as a "fact or fiction" set of statements designed to catch students' interest in a topic so that they are more attentive during a lecture (Cronin Jones, 2003). The reading is not specifically assigned. The assignment is to do the prediction guide. In doing the prediction guide, students must do the expected reading.

STANDARDS

This activity aligns with Science as Inquiry Standard 1: abilities necessary to do scientific inquiry and Science as Inquiry Standard 2: understandings about scientific inquiry. Scientific research often involves combing the literature and reading journal articles to obtain information that is relevant to an ongoing investigation. Scientists doing different kinds of research find it helpful to ask different kinds of questions.

THINKING SKILLS

Recalling, Investigating, Identifying, Defining, Matching

FOCUS ACTIVITY

The focus activity for the reading is doing the "ME" column in the prediction guide (see page 18). Tell students to complete the column by reading each statement and placing a "+" in front of a statement if they agree with it and a "0" if they disagree. A reproducible master of the prediction guide is on page 95.

OBJECTIVES

To gather information about a topic; to learn basic vocabulary and facts; to become more skillful readers of technical material.

INPUT

Explain to students that you want them to gather some information about a topic and learn its vocabulary. Tell them that the prediction guide will focus their attention on the important ideas in a reading selection. Explain that you will review and add to that information as you discuss the prediction guide with them after they have completed the "AUTHOR" column.

ACTIVITY

1. Distribute a copy of the prediction guide to each student. Tell students to fill in the "ME" column. Give them a few minutes to do so.

2. Tell students which sections or pages in their textbook include the information needed to complete the "AUTHOR" column.

3. Tell students to complete the "AUTHOR" column by placing a "+" in front of statements that agree with the text, placing a "0" in front of statements that disagree with the text, changing "0" statements so that they agree with the text, and noting the pages in the text where the information was found.

4. Tell students that they will be given the opportunity to share their information with the class as you lead the discussion of the prediction guide. They must understand that you expect them to do the reading and to be ready to participate in the discussion.

COGNITIVE DISCUSSION

Go over each item of the prediction guide. Help students organize notes about the material by outlining, mapping (see Chapter 20), or otherwise organizing information about the topic on the board, overhead projector, or interactive whiteboard.

Call on students to give their answers to the "AUTHOR" column. Ask them to read the original statement, tell whether the author agrees or disagrees with the statement, how they reworded "0" statements to make them agree with the text, and the number of the page where they found the information. Do not worry if a student answers incorrectly—he or she may have misunderstood the text. It is often difficult for students to understand everything they read in a textbook, and the prediction guide is your way of making sure that misunderstandings are corrected early on.

METACOGNITIVE DISCUSSION

Tell the students to do the following:

1. Write down at least two new facts or ideas about the topic they learned by doing the prediction guide. Remind them that they learned something new if they disagreed with the author when they filled in the "ME" column.

2. Write down one question that they still have about the topic that you are studying.

3. Complete a logging stem that asks them to create an analogy.

_____ is like_____ because . . .

For example,
Doing a prediction guide is like using a washing machine because . . .

CLOSURE AND ASSESSMENT

Closure: Help students connect the day's learning with prior knowledge by telling them how it relates to some information from daily life, a unit studied earlier in the year, or material they may have learned in another class. Divide students into groups of three and ask each group to discover another connection. Ask each group to write its connection on the board. Encourage students to record the connections in their logs.

Assessment: Tell students that they will be writing a prediction guide for an upcoming topic. Ask them the following questions: How will you identify key information or concepts found in a reading selection? How will you balance statements dealing with details and those focusing on key concepts (minnow and whale statements)? Tell them to each write answers to the questions, then have them share their answers with teammates. Have the small groups develop consensus answers to the questions, then lead a whole class discussion in which groups share their answers.

In the very near future, assign the writing of a prediction guide for a new topic. Tell students to bring a rough draft to class to share with their teammates, and have each small group write a prediction guide for the topic. Suggest that the best prediction guides consist of at least eight and no more than 12 statements. Review the individual and group products and share your thinking about the products with each group.

Prediction Guide: Fungi

(They are everywhere!)

Directions: Read each statement. Start with the "ME" column and place a "+" if you agree or a "0" if you disagree with the statement. Then read the textbook and decide whether or not the author agrees with the statement. Again use a "+" or a "0." Change all "0" statements so they agree with the textbook, and write down the number of the page where you found the information.

Me	Author	Statements
		A fungus does not make its own food.
		Most fungi can live on things that once were alive.
		Fungi must form spores to reproduce.
		Ringworm and athlete's foot are caused by fungi.
		All mushrooms are safe for us to eat.
		Fungi always harm the living things from which they get their food.
		Lichens are made up of a fungus and another organism.
		Lichens can live on rocks.
		We have not discovered any helpful fungi.
		Yeast is a form of fungus.
		Penicillin is made by a fungus.
		Fungi get their food from plants only.
		Fungi can live on clothing.

Prediction Guide: The Moon

(Is there a man in it? Is it made of green cheese? Did the cow jump over it?)

Directions: Read each statement. Start with the "ME" column and place a "+" if you agree or a "0" if you disagree with the statement. Then read the textbook and decide whether or not the author agrees with the statement. Again use a "+" or a "0." Change all "0" statements so they agree with the textbook, and write down the number of the page where you found the information.

Me	Author	Statements
		The moon has no atmosphere.
		Most of the moon's craters are very old.
		Surface temperatures on the moon do not get very high or very low.
		We see both sides of the moon from Earth.
		We would weigh just as much on the moon as we do on Earth.
		Moon rocks are light in color.
		Most of the moon's surface is covered with a fine dust.
		Shooting stars rarely hit the moon.
		The moon's gravity does not affect the Earth.
		During an eclipse, the Earth blocks sunlight from reaching the moon.

5

The Importance of Using Precise Labels

Latch Onto a Label

BACKGROUND

Quantitative information must often include labels (units of measurement) to make sense. Students often find calculations difficult because they do not include labels with the numbers that they are using. Some everyday examples may help them get the point.

STANDARDS

This activity aligns with Unifying Concepts and Processes Standard 3: change, constancy, and measurement and with Science as Inquiry Standard 1: abilities necessary to do scientific inquiry.

THINKING SKILLS

Identifying, Describing, Naming

FOCUS ACTIVITY

Do a think-pair-share. Ask students to identify a label that they paid attention to recently and why it is important to pay attention to labels. Record the shared answers on the board, overhead projector, or interactive whiteboard. Say that in science, the term *label* may be defined very narrowly as an identifying or descriptive marker that is attached to a measurement to indicate what property is being measured. Give a few examples: weight has *ounces* as a label; height may be labeled in *inches* or *feet*; numbers may be labeled as *pairs* or *dozens.*

OBJECTIVE

To include correct labels with quantitative information.

INPUT

Explain to students that when scientists talk about labeling data, they mean that correct units must accompany measurements. Measurements without labels communicate information imprecisely. In order to know the size or amount that a number describes, the number must be labeled.

ACTIVITY

Divide the class into groups of three. Each group needs a labeler, a conductor, and a scout. Each group will receive a list of ten statements that contain naked numbers (see page 23).

The labeler will be the person in the team whose clothes have the most labels on the outside. The labeler's job is to supply labels that make sense to the numbers that are naked. Give an example. What label or labels make sense in the following statement: "I will get to school on time even if I walk this morning. I only have to go four _____."

The conductor sits to the right of the labeler. The conductor watches the time and makes sure that everyone stays on task. The conductor also checks for agreement on the labels.

The scout's job begins when the labeler's job ends. The scout makes a copy of his or her group's labels and takes them to two other groups. He or she compares his or her group's labels with those of the other groups.

Groups will have 15 minutes to decide on their labels and 5 minutes to compare them with two other teams.

Ask a student to summarize the directions for the activity. Then give each group a copy of the unlabeled numbers worksheet.

COGNITIVE DISCUSSION

Make a list of the labels that were given to the naked numbers. Call on groups at random to tell you what labels were used. More than one label may be appropriate. Discuss with the class the communications problems that nonlabeling can cause.

Tell students that they now know what you mean when you tell them to label numbers. Stress the importance of including labels whenever they record quantitative information or use it in calculations.

METACOGNITIVE DISCUSSION

Have students complete the following stem in their logs:

Labeling a measurement is like letting paint dry because . . .

Have them answer these questions:

When do I find it easiest to remember to label numbers?

When do I find myself forgetting to latch onto labels?

How can I remember to attach labels to numbers?

Have students complete the log entry by summarizing the importance of careful labeling.

CLOSURE AND ASSESSMENT

Closure: Set up 10 to 12 stations with a different measurement task at each station. Provide the instructions and equipment for the task at each station. Have teams rotate through all of the stations, making and recording their measurements, and checking for correct use of labels. Include a complete mix of measurements of mass, volume, length, and time (how long does it take a teammate to walk a given distance, for example). As teams work, rotate among them and check their measurements for correct labeling.

Assessment: Check students' notes from hands-on activities for correct use of labels throughout the year.

Latch Onto a Label:
The Importance of Using Precise Labels

Directions: Fill in the label or labels that make sense.

1. I cannot carry that pile of books home! It must weigh 40 _____.

2. Wait for me! I can finish this report in two _____.

3. We will be tired when we get to the beach. It will take us seven _____ to get there.

4. It will be a big party, so I had better get five _____ of juice.

5. That rock hit the ground awfully hard! Bet it weighs one _____.

6. I am glad that project is done! It took me three _____ to complete it!

7. There will only be two of us for dinner. One _____ of hamburger meat will be plenty.

8. What do you mean we ran out of hot dog buns! We bought six _____.

9. Let's paint the house. It looks like we will need about 12 _____ of paint.

10. Here's a ten-dollar bill. Go to the store and get four _____ of milk. You will not have much change!

6

Think-Pair-Share

And the Answer Is . . .

BACKGROUND

Many students hesitate volunteering to answer questions in the classroom. Volunteering is a high-risk way to reply to a teacher's questions. It is much safer to wait for Johnny or Judy who always knows the right answers anyway. Think-pair-share lowers the risk by giving each student a partner with whom he or she can discuss a question and agree on the answer.

STANDARDS

This activity aligns with Unifying Concepts and Processes Standard 2: evidence, models, and explanations. Think-pair-share asks students to generate answers by drawing on and interpreting prior knowledge or information.

THINKING SKILLS

Identifying, Describing, Listing, Defining

FOCUS ACTIVITY

Ask students "what is a synonym for *think?*" Call on students at random to share their answers. Record their answers on the board, overhead, chart paper, or interactive whiteboard.

OBJECTIVES

To increase student participation in the learning process; to improve their recall, verbal communication skills, and the quality of answers.

INPUT

It is vital to explain the strategy to students before using it for the first time. They will not know what to do without some instruction. Complete instructions for the strategy are detailed in the Activity section.

ACTIVITY

1. Tell students to *listen* while you ask them a question. You may repeat the question to be sure that they heard it correctly.

2. Tell students to (silently and individually) think of several answers to the question. Tell them how long they will have to think. Questions that involve simple answers may require 7 to 10 seconds of think time. More complex questions will require as much as one minute. Encourage them to jot down a few notes about their answers.

3. Next, cue students to pair with a neighbor and discuss their answers. During this discussion, pairs will develop a consensus answer. Pair time will vary with the complexity of the answer. Encourage pairs to record their answers as they develop with discussion.

4. Finally, ask pairs to share their answers with the whole class. You may ask for volunteers or call on pairs in a wraparound. List or web (see Chapter 1) all of the different answers on the board, overhead, chart paper, or interactive whiteboard. As you list an answer, say "Thank you" or repeat the student's answer. Your acknowledgment of student answers must be value-free if the process is to work successfully next time.

5. You may use verbal, visual, or audio cues to move students from one step to the next. Teachers often use bells, hand signals, light signals, or the words think-pair–get-ready-to-share. Explain the cues to your students before you use the process for the first time. Remind them of the cues until they are used to them.

6. While students are thinking and pairing, observe them closely. Watch and listen. Jot down your observations.

COGNITIVE DISCUSSION

Examine the answers after they are all recorded. This is the time to modify or expand on those that need it or to eliminate any that the class (with your guidance) agrees are incorrect. The activity will generate a number of definitions for *"think,"* so do a follow-up think-pair-share. Ask, "How many definitions, on average, do you find when you look up a word in the dictionary?"

Collect these answers and ask, "How can you decide which answer is the most accurate estimate?" Gather answers by doing another think-pair-share.

METACOGNITIVE DISCUSSION

Ask students to write a log entry about something new that they learned or a surprising point of view contributed by one of the pairs.

One new thing I learned today is . . .

I was surprised to hear . . .

Tell them to continue the log entry by analyzing their level of comfort in volunteering an answer as a member of a pair.

It was easy (difficult) for me to volunteer my answers because . . .

Tell them to finish the entry by describing how they will improve the next time the strategy is used.

The next time I use think-pair-share, I want to . . .

CLOSURE AND ASSESSMENT

Closure: Share some of your observations with students. Tell them what you saw and heard that showed their understanding of the process. You may suggest improvements, but be sure to let them know what worked well. *Catch them being good at thinking!*

Assessment: Use think-pair-share to break up lectures by stopping the delivery of new information and asking students to identify or explain one or more key pieces of information or big ideas contained in the lecture. Taking time to do a think-pair-share every 7 to 10 minutes will help students stay focused on the lecture and it will help them remember the content. Or use a think-pair-share to collect ideas about everyday phenomena that connect to science content. If a biology unit includes information about the response of green plants to light, hold up a piece of curly bamboo and ask, "How do you think the growers make the bamboo curl like that?" If a chemistry lesson focuses on factors that affect the speed of reactions, display two clear glass containers, one holding steaming water and the other holding room temperature water, and before adding drops of food coloring ask, "In which container will the color spread out faster?"

Each time you do think-pair-share, make notes in your log about the comfort level of your students and the quality of their answers.

7

Making Observations

It Makes Cents to Me

BACKGROUND

Skillful observing is vital to progress in science. Students must become aware of the importance of making careful, accurate observations using all of their senses (unless tasting and touching are unsafe). Some outstanding discoveries have resulted from serendipitous observations—aspirin, aspartame, and sticky note glue are three that are frequently cited.

The "blind" coin identification that students do in this activity is based on a neurological test that was included in military physical exams in the 1940s. One of my college professors was given this exam, and he introduced me to its use.

STANDARDS

This activity aligns with Unifying Concepts and Processes Standard 1: systems, order, and organization and with Unifying Concepts and Processes Standard 3: change, constancy, and measurement. Because students are familiar with the monetary system, they will understand the relationship among the three coins that they are describing and identifying. They develop an appreciation for the importance of making detailed observations by the time they complete the activity.

THINKING SKILLS

Observing, Describing, Identifying, Matching

FOCUS ACTIVITY

Using think-pair-share, ask students to list the five senses and to describe specific information that each of the senses can give them about an object. Web their "share" answers on the board, overhead, chart paper, or interactive whiteboard.

OBJECTIVES

To make accurate observations using all five senses; to check each other's observations for accuracy. These observations may include qualitative and quantitative information.

INPUT

Review the "share" web after recording all answers. Revise the web as needed.

Tell students, "I think you're familiar with money. I think you think it's easy to tell coins apart. We'll find out just how easy it is by doing this activity."

ACTIVITY

1. Divide students into groups of three. Each group needs an *observer* who will use the five senses to make observations and measurements, a *recorder* who will write down the observations, and a *guide* who will time the activity and let the group know when it is time to rotate roles and who will check with group members for agreement on the accuracy of observations at the end of the round.

2. The activity will take place in three initial rounds and three final rounds. Roles rotate one person to the right with each new round, so each person gets a chance to play each role for an initial round and again in a final round.

3. The objects to be observed are a penny, a nickel, and a dime. Each observer is to make as many observations about the objects as possible in one minute. The recorder and the guide may not help the observer.

4. The first-round guide is the person who lives closest to school. The first-round observer sits to the right of the guide. The first-round recorder is the third group member.

5. Be sure that all groups know who has which role for the first round.

6. Check for accuracy in understanding the instructions. Have a student repeat them.

7. Tell the first-round observers to come to your desk for the three coins.

8. When all groups have their coins, start the initial rounds.

9. At the conclusion of the three initial rounds, signal for silence. Tell the students that they are now going to check the accuracy of their observations. The

observer in the initial round will reclaim the coins. The observer will then be blindfolded and will have one minute to examine the coins and identify the dime. The observer will know if the identification was accurate as soon he or she removes the blindfold. Whether the selection is correct or not, the observer is not to let teammates know how the identification was made.

10. The roles will rotate as before. There will be three final rounds. Each group will keep score of the successful identifications—how many final-round observers correctly select the dime.

12. Do the final rounds. Observe groups as the "blindfolded" observers make their selections and check their accuracy.

COGNITIVE DISCUSSION

Do a wraparound in which you ask each group to tell you one unique property about each type of coin and one property that all three have in common. Record the observations in a web or map.

METACOGNITIVE DISCUSSION

Ask students to respond to the following questions in their logs:

1. Why did you think you had the dime?

2. Was your identification accurate? Did the accuracy of your identification surprise you?

3. What might you do differently next time?

4. What did you learn about observing with all of your senses?

Have students share their answers with others in their group.

Do a wraparound. Ask each group for its most interesting or amusing response to the questions.

CLOSURE AND ASSESSMENT

Closure: Tell students that you are going to analyze the effectiveness of their observation skills. Ask them to do a log entry describing the school as seen from the street in front of the school. Take a "field trip" so that students can check their observations against the actual appearance of the school, and tell students to record the results of the check in their logs.

Assessment: Periodically, check the quality of observations that students make about the materials or phenomena involved in a hands-on activity. Look for observations and measurements that indicate use of at least the senses of sight, sound, and smell. Encourage continuous improvement in each student's observations.

8

Accurate Observations

Hide in Plain Sight

BACKGROUND

Remind students of the importance of being skillful, accurate observers.

STANDARDS

This activity aligns with Unifying Concepts and Processes Standard 2: evidence, models, and explanations, and with Unifying Concepts and Processes Standard 3: change, constancy, and measurement. Scientists need to be able to identify changes in materials, in test subjects, and in their environment. To do this, they need to be careful observers. In this activity, students will be tested to see if they can identify a changing feature of the classroom.

THINKING SKILLS

Observing, Describing, Identifying, Matching

FOCUS ACTIVITY

Tell students that you are at that moment checking their powers of observation. Tell them that they have five days in which to figure out how you are doing this.

OBJECTIVE

To make accurate observations about one's surroundings.

INPUT

Tell students that their powers of observation are being tested daily in your class. Tell them to write you a note when they have discovered the test and to record their observations about the observation test in their logs. Do not tell them anything else.

ACTIVITY

Get a small but noticeable stuffed or rubber animal. Hang it someplace in your classroom where students can see it. Have it in place before you do the focus activity. Move it to a new location each day. Keep track of each location of the animal. Collect and check off notes as students figure out what you are doing. (I did this with a small stuffed mole, and I was amazed at how many of my high school chemistry students needed four or five days to notice the daily changes in position. A physics teacher friend used a rubber snake that he placed on top of a suspended ceiling tile. At the beginning of the test period, only the snake's head was visible. Each day a few more inches of the snake emerged from the ceiling. By the end of the test, the snake was almost falling out of the ceiling, and some students still had not noticed the change in its positioning.)

On the sixth day, announce that the test is over. Have a student tell what the test was.

COGNITIVE DISCUSSION

Divide the class into groups of three. Have each group write or sketch the test day by day. Where was the animal each day?

The final product is a map showing the day-by-day location of the animal.

METACOGNITIVE DISCUSSION

Read your record of the animal locations to the class. Tell groups to check their accuracy against your record as you read it to them.

Tell students to write a log entry analyzing the accuracy of their observations. Ask them to describe how the activity made them better observers.

Have students use a web or a "Top 10 List" to record: Ten Reasons Why I *Know* I Pay Attention to the Location of Objects in my Surroundings *or* Ten Reasons Why I *Know* I Do *Not* Pay Attention to the Location of Objects in my Surroundings.

Do a wraparound, asking students to tell you how the activity made them better observers. Record their answers.

CLOSURE AND ASSESSMENT

Closure: Give each group a photo showing a physical feature of the school. Make sure that this is a feature that does not change. The photo needs to show enough of the school feature to make identification possible. Choose school features that are located in common areas, and show only a part of a feature in each photograph. Tell groups, "You have three days to locate the feature shown in your photograph and to sketch a map of the school showing the location of the feature."

Assessment: After three days, hold a class discussion during which each group identifies the school feature shown in its photograph, describes the location of the feature, and relates the process that the group used to identify the feature.

PART II

Processing Information

9

Mental Modeling

What Is Behind Door Number Two?

BACKGROUND

Every scientific field involves the use of mental models to picture things that we cannot observe directly. Astronomers model the solar system and the universe; chemists model the atom; biologists model the structure of DNA. Students need to understand the processes that are involved in building these mental models.

STANDARDS

This activity aligns with Science as Inquiry Standard 1: abilities necessary to do scientific inquiry. It requires students to make careful observations and measurements and to hypothesize.

THINKING SKILLS

Observing, Modeling, Analyzing, Synthesizing, Making Analogies

FOCUS ACTIVITY

Ask students what goes through their minds when they hear the word *model*. Do a think-pair-share. Web responses on the blackboard, overhead, or big paper. Explain that a scientific model is a picture of something that is very difficult to observe directly. Some models of very small objects, like atoms, are drawn entirely from indirect observation and are changed as new observations are made. The model is an attempt by scientists to picture very large or very small objects.

OBJECTIVE

To develop a model of something that is hidden.

You need to do some advance preparation for this lesson. Obtain several semi-opaque plastic boxes—about 10" x 4" x 4"—one for each group of three students. You can pick up boxes like this very inexpensively at any hardware store or discount store with a hardware department. (I have also used cardboard boxes, but they do not work as well. I also have a "road show" set of observation boxes for which I've used the plastic canisters that hold fresh 35 mm film. These work very well. Their contents must be smaller objects such as a single coin or nut or bolt, a few small beads, a small button or two, bits of cotton or Styrofoam, and so on.)

Use a punch to make holes in two opposite sides of the boxes. The holes need to align so that students can explore the interior of the boxes using a long, thin piece of dowel rod.

Fill the boxes as follows:

Box 1: several nuts, bolts, washers, and so forth

Box 2: a short length of chain

Box 3: a few handfuls of assorted buttons

Box 4: a dozen or so clothespins

Box 5: several empty spools from thread

Box 6: several bottle or jar caps

Box 7: a dozen or so pencils (old stubs without erasers are fine)

Box 8: cotton balls—really pack them in tight

Box 9: Styrofoam noodles—really pack them in tight

Box 10: newspaper—really pack it in tight

Seal the boxes with masking tape.

After the focus activity, tell students that they are going to make some observations about some objects that you have hidden in a box and develop a model of the hidden objects.

ACTIVITY

1. Divide the class into groups of three. Each group needs a recorder, model maker, and guide (to watch the time).

2. Tell the class that each group will receive a sealed box.

3. The job of each group is to make observations about the hidden contents of the box and to develop a model that pictures the possible contents of the box. The model can be very specific; they can give the name of the object that they believe is in the box.

4. Group members are to rotate roles about every 90 seconds. Each group member will have a chance to perform each role.

5. A group may not open or damage the box in any way. A group may hold its box in front of a strong light source to see if that gives any information about the contents of the box.

6. Each group will describe its model of the box contents to the rest of the class before any of the boxes are opened.

7. Be sure that students understand the instructions. Ask a student, selected at random, to repeat them.

8. Begin the activity.

COGNITIVE DISCUSSION

After groups have investigated their boxes for 10 minutes or so, call time. Have each group describe its model of the contents of its box. Record the descriptions.

Ask each group if using the light source gave them any useful information. If the boxes are made of thin plastic, using the strong light source will produce an outline of larger, denser contents. Ask students where this kind of information collecting can be encountered in everyday life. Using energy to penetrate the human body is the basis for different types of medical diagnostic imaging.

Open the boxes. Ask each group to comment on how closely its model describes the contents of its box.

METACOGNITIVE DISCUSSION

Have each group answer these questions about the activity:

1. What were we asked to do?

2. How well were we able to do it?

3. What else could we do to develop more accurate models?

4. What did we learn about the process of developing mental pictures of things that cannot be directly observed?

CLOSURE AND ASSESSMENT

Closure: Have each group read its answer to the last question aloud. Emphasize the difficulty that scientists have in trying to develop models of things that are very large, very small, or very far away.

Assessment: Have each student write a short essay or produce a storyboard (see Chapter 19) describing how he or she could examine a wrapped present to guess what's in the box. As you score the essays, make a list of unique ideas to share with the class. Students may suggest that the gift-giver is known for a certain type of present. The size of the package, its shape, its heaviness or lightness, the way the box sounds when shaken, the occasion of the gift, and the time of year it is given may all be suggested by students. Look for ways in which the in-class activity influenced the thinking behind each essay.

10

Becoming Better Listeners

What a Bright Idea

BACKGROUND

Good ideas and discoveries often come from brainstorming sessions in which large numbers of ideas are generated. These ideas must be offered in a safe-risk setting—put downs are not allowed. In the real world, ideas are evaluated and kept or rejected only after the initial brainstorming has occurred.

STANDARDS

This activity aligns with Unifying Concepts and Processes Standard 3: change, constancy, and measurement, and with Standard 4: evolution and equilibrium. It asks students to brainstorm ways to change a given product or procedure and to predict the ways in which that change will affect the behavior or usefulness of what is being changed. It asks students to recognize that the effects of changes can be observed and evaluated.

THINKING SKILLS

Active Listening, Generating Ideas, Analyzing, Comparing, Explaining Why

FOCUS ACTIVITY

Tell students that before Columbus sailed, he was told, "The earth is flat! You will fall off the edge!" Ask volunteers to contribute other famous historical put downs.

OBJECTIVES

To practice generating ideas in a safe-risk environment; to practice responding to others' ideas in a positive way.

INPUT

Remind students of the DOVE guidelines (see the reproducible master on page 90).

ACTIVITY

1. Divide the class into groups of three.

2. Tell each group to brainstorm a list of ten things that give off light and to wait for further instructions. Tell them to be sure that the group has a recorder to write down the list.

3. As groups finish their lists, give each group a randomly chosen number that corresponds to one of the items on the list. Have the recorder circle that item.

4. Each group now needs an idea person and a predictor. The recorder will keep his or her role for the time being.

5. The idea person, sitting to the recorder's right, is to suggest an improvement to the light-generating item that was circled.

6. The predictor is to say to the idea person, "That improvement is a good idea because. . . ."

7. The recorder is to write down the improvement and the prediction.

8. The roles then rotate one person to the right. The activity proceeds until each person has had two turns at being the idea person.

9. The group is then to do a graphic that shows their improved light-giving device. Each member of the group must be able to explain the graphic.

10. When all of the graphics are finished, have each group present its graphic to the class.

11. Decorate the room with the graphics.

COGNITIVE DISCUSSION

Ask students to write a log entry in which they describe the requirements that must be met for an object to produce light. Ask students to use a fishbone graphic organizer (see Chapter 12) to list activities that may be done with fairly low light, activities that require moderate light, and activities that require very bright light. Then ask them to suggest sources of light for each type of activity.

METACOGNITIVE DISCUSSION

Have each group answer these questions:

1. How did this activity promote our creativity and enhance our predicting skills?

2. How did the brainstorming guidelines help us do our job well?

3. When could we use this process again?

CLOSURE AND ASSESSMENT

Closure: Ask students to write a log entry describing a place where or a time when they could use their improved light-giving device.

Assessment: Repeat the activity, this time asking students to generate ideas to answer a question or solve a problem related to everyday life such as: "What are the environmental implications of using standard incandescent light bulbs. What are some alternative light sources?" "When you check out at the grocery store, do you ask for paper, plastic, or do you prefer some other packaging? What are the advantages and disadvantages to each choice?" "What is the source of electricity used by this school? What are some alternate sources and how might you convince the school board that looking into these alternatives is a good idea?" Score answers using a rubric that you have given students before they do the writing assignment, and suggest that they use the rubric to self-evaluate and revise their work.

11

The Venn Diagram

Frogs and Salamanders

BACKGROUND

The Venn diagram is an old visual tool for comparing and contrasting that has its roots in philosophy. When new math sprang onto the scene, using Venn diagrams was very popular in all content areas. That popularity faded for a while, but use of the Venn diagram has revived because it is a very effective way to organize information.

STANDARDS

This activity aligns with Unifying Concepts and Processes Standard 1: Systems, order, and organization. The use of the Venn diagram gives students a way to organize information about related organisms or objects so that they can clearly see the similarities and differences between them.

THINKING SKILLS

Comparing, Contrasting, Analyzing, Distinguishing

FOCUS ACTIVITY

Ask students to give you some synonyms for the word *characteristics* (or *attributes*). Do a think-pair-share. Record shared answers on the board, overhead, chart paper, or an interactive whiteboard. Hold up a textbook and a notebook. Ask students to find similarities and differences in the two objects. Suggest that they write down their answers in their logs.

Call on students at random. Ask each student to give you one way in which the books are similar and one way in which they are different. Record their answers.

OBJECTIVES

To compare and contrast objects using a Venn diagram to organize the information. To understand that related items also possess unique attributes.

INPUT

Find another teacher who will be your partner. (If you have trouble finding a teacher who can join your class, ask for a student volunteer.) Draw the Venn circles on the blackboard. Label the circles.

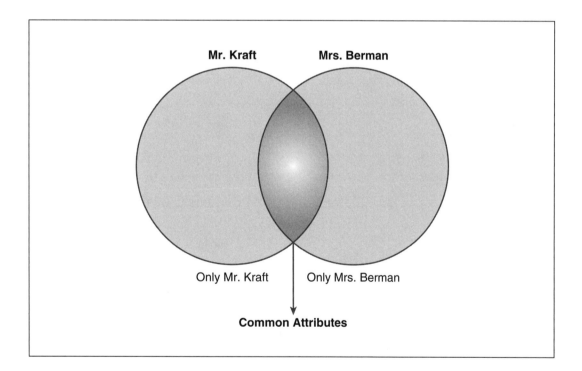

Ask one student, called on at random, to name one unique characteristic of your partner (Mr. Kraft). Ask another student to name one of your own unique attributes. Ask a third student to name an attribute that you and your colleague share. Record their answers in the appropriate sections of the Venn diagram. Continue for a few more rounds. Students will quickly catch on and have fun learning to Venn by using attributes of their teachers.

ACTIVITY

1. Divide students into groups of three. Give each group a large sheet of paper, a pizza pan or cardboard pizza circle, and three different colored markers.

2. Explain to students that they are to use the pizza pans to draw circles for a Venn diagram. It will help them see what is going on if each circle is a different color.

3. Give each group one copy of the "Frogs and Salamanders" reading (see box) or assign a similar section in your science textbook.

Frogs and Salamanders

Frogs and salamanders are amphibians. All amphibians are cold-blooded—their body temperatures adjust to the temperatures of their surroundings. Amphibians must lay their eggs in water because the eggs will dry out on land and because the hatchlings breathe with gills, just like fish! Adult amphibians breathe with lungs, so they can live on land.

Frogs have four legs. The two front legs are small and the two back legs are large and powerful. The large back legs allow frogs to jump long distances. Frogs have long, sticky tongues that they use to catch the insects they eat. Frogs have no tails. Adult frogs have no gills.

Salamanders have four legs of about equal size. They also have long tails. Some kinds of salamanders keep their gills and live in water for their whole lives.

---

4. Tell students that their job is to organize the information from the reading using a Venn diagram. Supervise the drawing and labeling of the circles.

5. Give students a reasonable time limit. Ten minutes is plenty for the sample reading.

6. Post the results.

COGNITIVE DISCUSSION

Have students do a log entry in which they summarize what they learned about the two organisms or objects. Ask them not to refer to the assigned reading or the Venn diagram in their log entry. Then have them compare their summaries with the information in the Venn diagram produced by their group and correct the log entries as needed.

METACOGNITIVE DISCUSSION

Ask students to summarize how they did the task. First, have them write log entries; then lead a class discussion. Point out differences in thinking styles that are reflected in different approaches to the task.

Ask students to continue the log entry by recording how their teammates helped them with the task.

CLOSURE AND ASSESSMENT

Closure: Ask students if they can think of other pairs of objects that they can compare and contrast using a Venn diagram. Have them write their ideas in their logs. Then do a wraparound, asking randomly selected students for ideas. Record their answers on the board, overhead, or chart paper.

Assessment: Before students do a writing assignment in which they compare and contrast related items, have them organize the information using a Venn diagram. As they gain skill in using the graphic organizer, you may decide to have them do some three-way comparisons. Sample graphic organizers can be found online at a number of web sites including: http://www.edhelper.com/teachers/Sorting_graphic_organizers.htm. Use a checklist (see reproducible on page 98) to assess how effectively and skillfully students use the Venn diagram, and ask students to self-evaluate their proficiency.

12

Using a Fishbone

The Planets Organized

BACKGROUND

A fishbone graphic organizer looks like its name. It can be used in a number of ways. In this activity, a fishbone will be used to organize information about the planets in our solar system.

STANDARDS

This activity aligns with Unifying Concepts and Processes Standard 1: systems, order, and organization. Use of the fishbone graphic organizer encourages students to pattern information about the topic they are studying.

THINKING SKILLS

Organizing , Analyzing, Sorting, Distinguishing

FOCUS ACTIVITY

Hold up a pen, a pencil, a piece of chalk, and a marker. Ask students to start thinking about attributes of the four objects.

Draw a fishbone graphic organizer on the blackboard, overhead, chart paper, or interactive whiteboard. Label the fishbone as shown.

Explain to students that the angled bones are used for main categories and the horizontal bones are used for details within each category.

Fill in the fishbone with attributes of the writing tools. Call on students for ideas.

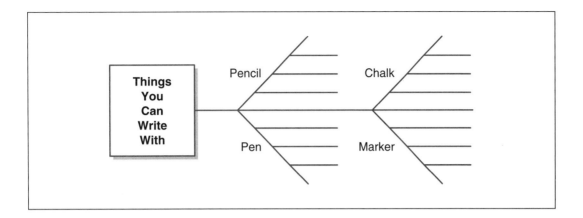

OBJECTIVE

To organize attributes or characteristics of the planets in our solar system using a fishbone graphic organizer.

INPUT

Remind students of the meaning of *attributes* or *characteristics*. If you saved your list of synonyms from the focus activity in Chapter 11, "Frogs and Salamanders," this would be a good time to pull it out and share it with the class.

Tell students that they will be organizing attributes of planets in the solar system using a fishbone. Ask them how many main angled bones they will need. Be sure that they know how to set up the fishbone—the head is the title (The Solar System) and the angled bones are labeled with the main topics (names of the planets).

ACTIVITY

1. Divide the students into groups of three.

2. Each group will need a recorder, checker, and reader.

3. Give each group a reading passage that summarizes the attributes of each of the planets in the solar system. Most earth science books contain a section that does this in just a few pages.

4. Give each group a large sheet of paper, a straightedge, and assorted markers. Have them draw and label the outline of the fishbone. Supervise this closely. The head is labeled "The Solar System" and there is a main (angled) bone for each planet.

5. Give students time to fill in details about each planet on the fishbone.

6. Post the results.

COGNITIVE DISCUSSION

Have students write a log entry that summarizes the information that they organized about the planets. They are to write without consulting the reading or the fishbone. Completed log entries are then checked against the fishbone and corrected as needed.

METACOGNITIVE DISCUSSION

Ask students to log their responses to these questions:

1. What were we asked to do?

2. What did we do well?

3. Summarize the process that was used and think about how you would do it differently next time.

4. What did you learn?

Have group members share their individual log entries with one another.

CLOSURE AND ASSESSMENT

Closure: Ask groups to brainstorm other situations in which they can use a fishbone to organize information. Call on groups to share their ideas with the rest of the class. Record the ideas. Suggest that this technique can be especially helpful to organize information during review of a topic before a test.

Assessment: Keep a personal record of the fishbone situations suggested by students, and when such situations or topics arise during the semester, monitor how students organize information to see whether they remember to use the fishbone graphic organizer. Ask students to review their information-organizing strategies to self-evaluate their comfort and facility with this tool.

Extensions: Every science discipline presents opportunities for students to use this graphic organizer. Physics students may use a fishbone to organize information about different forms of energy or simple machines. In chemistry, students can use it to systematize their thinking about states of matter or families of elements. Biology students can use the fishbone to arrange and order information about plant or animal families or individual species within a family.

13

One Way to Use a Matrix

That Is My Pet Matrix

BACKGROUND

The ability to list or describe the attributes of items is crucial to good critical thinking. Only by recognizing the attributes of something can we distinguish that item from others and recognize it when we encounter it again.

STANDARDS

This activity aligns with Unifying Concepts and Processes Standard 1: systems, order, and organization, and with Science as Inquiry Standard 1: abilities necessary to do scientific inquiry. A matrix is an excellent tool for organizing and displaying large numbers of observations and measurements in such a way that the information can be quickly reviewed and analyzed.

THINKING SKILLS

Analyzing, Organizing Information, Classifying, Distinguishing, Sorting

FOCUS ACTIVITY

Do a think-pair-share in which you ask students to name a synonym for *classify*. Record the shared responses on the blackboard, overhead, chart paper, or interactive whiteboard.

OBJECTIVE

To identify the attributes that can be used to identify items.

INPUT

Remind students that they may use all of their senses and a variety of measuring techniques and tools to determine the attributes of items. Suggest that there may be times when they choose not to use one of the senses. Draw the following matrix on the board or overhead, and tell students that you are asking them to learn how to use this tool by organizing the attributes of some possibly familiar animals.

Attributes						
Pets	*Size*	*Skin covering*	*Warm- or cold-blooded*	*Legs (?)*	*Other appendages*	*Food*
Dog						
Cat						
Fish						
Bird						
Other						
Other						

Ask students to suggest other attributes that may be useful in identifying a kind of pet and in distinguishing one kind of pet from another: bedding, shelter, teeth, and odor are some possibilities.

ACTIVITY

1. Divide students into groups of three. Each group needs a recorder, checker, and scout. The scout may leave the group to get materials—big paper and markers—and to trade information about attributes with other groups. The recorder will draw the matrix on the big paper and fill in group answers. The checker will poll group members to be sure that agreement has been reached before an answer is recorded in the matrix.

2. Each group will fill in the matrix completely. Emphasize that some discussion may be necessary before an answer is recorded for a type of pet. Stress that such discussion results in the sharing of unique information that each member brings to the activity and that group members must focus on answers that are complete and accurate. Remind students to criticize or critique ideas, not people. Each individual is to be treated with respect.

3. Ask a student to repeat the instructions.

4. Give the groups 30 minutes to set up and fill in a matrix on a large sheet of paper.

COGNITIVE DISCUSSION

Post and discuss the matrices. Ask each group to describe a lively discussion it had about one of the attributes for one type of pet.

METACOGNITIVE DISCUSSION

Ask groups to decide how they could use the matrix in another class—English, math, social studies, physical education. Call on each group to share one answer with the rest of the class. Record the answers. If time permits, do another wrap-around.

CLOSURE AND ASSESSMENT

Closure: Have students write a log entry in which they define *attribute* and *classify* and describe the usefulness of organizing information in a matrix. Ask them to discuss how using a matrix would be helpful in identifying a new example of one of the types of pets included in the matrix.

Assessment: Give students a new group of related items and tell them to organize information about those items using a matrix. In biology, they may organize information about plant or animal species. Physics students can use a matrix to systematize their thinking about simple machines or the ways in which surfaces interact with light. A matrix can help chemistry students arrange and develop information about behavior of elements, classes of organic compounds, or types of chemical changes.

Assess the effectiveness and accuracy with which students use the matrix.

14

Looking for Attributes

Scavenger Hunt

BACKGROUND

An object may be much more than it seems to be. Students can sharpen their imaginations and prediction skills by looking at objects in new ways.

STANDARDS

This activity aligns with Unifying Concepts and Processes Standard 1: systems, order, and organization, and with Unifying Concepts and Processes Standard 5: form and function. Students need to use the functions of each member of a collection of objects to propose ways of organizing the objects into groups. The sorting and classifying will help students understand the creation of classes of items.

THINKING SKILLS

Analyzing, Predicting (function), Classifying, Comparing, Sorting

FOCUS ACTIVITY

Hold up a pen, a baster, and a cardboard tube from a roll of paper towels or toilet paper. Do a think-pair-share by asking students to name an attribute that all three have in common. Record shared answers on the board, overhead projector, or interactive whiteboard.

OBJECTIVE

To find attributes, properties, or functions that can be used to group objects in common or uncommon ways.

INPUT

Draw a fishbone graphic organizer (see Chapter 12) on the board, overhead, or interactive whiteboard. Remind students that the angled bones are labeled with the names of major categories and the horizontal bones are used for details. In this activity, the major categories are the attributes or functions that are used to form groups of objects and the details are the objects that fit each attribute. For example, the pen, baster, and cardboard tube are all objects that are hollow, or objects that roll, objects that can be filled, or whatever other attributes or functions pairs of students name in the focus activity.

ACTIVITY

The day before doing this activity, tell students that their homework for the next class is to bring four small objects from home. All four must fit easily into one sandwich bag.

1. Divide the class into groups of three. Each group needs a recorder, conductor, and sorter. The activity will have three rounds. Roles rotate one person to the right with each round.

2. The person in the group who brought the smallest object will be the first-round sorter. The job of the sorter is to pool all of the objects brought by group members and then to sort out groups of two, three, or four objects that have a common attribute. The sorter is to name the attribute or function that he or she used in putting together each group of objects. The sorter is to find as many groups of two, three, or four objects as he or she can in one minute.

3. The recorder is the person to the right of the sorter. The recorder writes each function or attribute named by the sorter on an angled fishbone and records the names of the objects with a given attribute on the horizontal bones.

4. The conductor watches the clock and tells the group when it is time for the roles to rotate.

5. The conductor and the recorder may not help the sorter.

6. Give each group a sheet of large paper and markers or a copy of a fishbone graphic organizer. (You may use the reproducible master on page 97.)

7. Ask a member of the class to repeat the instructions. Remind students that they may look at objects in uncommon ways when determining attributes.

8. Help the conductors watch the one-minute time limit as groups do the activity.

COGNITIVE DISCUSSION

Draw a fishbone graphic organizer on the blackboard or interactive whiteboard. Ask each group for its most interesting attribute and the objects that fit that attribute. Record the answers on the board. Post the group fishbones.

Ask students, "How did you think about form and function when you were making your groups or classes of objects? What differences did you notice in the two approaches to grouping objects? How does form suggest function? How does function follow form?" Have students brainstorm answers in small groups, and then lead a whole class discussion to develop answers to the questions.

METACOGNITIVE DISCUSSION

Have each group answer the questions below. The final recorder will write the consensus answers and all group members will sign the product.

1. What were we asked to do?

2. What did we do well?

3. What would we do differently next time?

4. What did we learn about looking at objects for uncommon attributes?

CLOSURE AND ASSESSMENT

Closure: Have each individual write a log entry:

This activity was fun and helped me stretch my imagination because . . .

Looking at common and uncommon ways to group items is important because . . .

Here's what I learned about the relationship between form and function . . .

Assessment: Suggest to students that identifying common or complimentary functions among items is a vital component of understanding systems. Ask them to find and organize information about common or complimentary functions of items in systems in a science discipline. Biology students may investigate an ecosystem or a body system. In physics, students may explore energy transmission systems or optical systems. Chemistry students may organize information about basic particles of matter or systems of chemical bonding. In earth science, students may investigate geologic fault systems or solar systems.

PART III

Analyzing and Applying Information

15

Lateral Thinking

Cook's Choice

BACKGROUND

Lateral thinking, invented by Dr. Edward de Bono, forces students to look at ideas and objects in new and different ways. It can be used to improve understanding or to develop new ways of solving problems. However it is used, lateral thinking generates exciting discussions in the classroom.

STANDARDS

This activity aligns with Unifying Concepts and Processes Standard 1: systems, order, and organization, and with Unifying Concepts and Processes Standard 2: evidence, models, and explanation. Students model the digestive and excretory systems using familiar kitchen tools, examine the interrelationships among the various organs in the two systems, and predict problems that result from poor functioning of one or more of those organs.

THINKING SKILL

Generating Ideas, Imagining, Idealizing, Speculating

FOCUS ACTIVITY

Do a think-pair-share. Ask students, "What is one way in which digesting food is like cooking food?" Record shared answers on the blackboard, overhead, chart paper, or an interactive whiteboard.

OBJECTIVE

To generate ideas through lateral thinking that will improve understanding of the way in which the digestive system works.

INPUT

Ask students to recall the DOVE guidelines (see the DOVE guidelines in the reproducibles section of this book, page 90). Call on students at random to tell you what each of the letters stands for. Ask them why it is important to use the DOVE guidelines when they are brainstorming together.

ACTIVITY

1. Divide the class into groups of three.

2. Tell the groups that their job will be to design a graphic that shows the human digestive and excretory systems as a series of interconnected kitchen utensils.

3. Have each group brainstorm a list of utensils.

4. Each utensil is to be used for an appropriate purpose. For instance, students would not use a baster to cut or shred food or use a blender to separate a mixture of foods.

5. A utensil may be used for a nontraditional purpose. For example, students may choose to use a rolling pin to crush food or a sifter to separate large from small pieces of food.

6. The parts of the digestive and excretory systems are to be shown in order. Food is taken in at the mouth and solid waste passes out from the large intestine. Dissolved wastes are excreted using a separate pathway. Utensils must be connected in the same order as the organs that they represent.

7. The utensils are to be labeled with the name of the part of the digestive and excretory systems that each represents.

8. The graphic is to be done on big paper.

9. Set a time limit for completion of the graphic. Thirty minutes is a good idea.

10. Check to see if there are any questions. Ask a student, chosen at random, to repeat the instructions.

11. The assigned roles within each group are: the conductor, who keeps an eye on the time and keeps the group on task; the encourager, who maintains the confidence of the group; and the gopher, who gets the big paper and markers and who returns the markers to their proper place. Group members may decide among themselves who will do the drawing and coloring. (A group may decide, for example, to have one student do the drawing lightly in pencil and the others color in the sketches while the artist moves on to a new portion of the graphic.)

12. Have each group present its completed graphic to the class.

COGNITIVE DISCUSSION

Ask students to make a log entry identifying the most important role of each of the major organs in the digestive and excretory systems. Tell them to use a bulleted list, a fishbone graphic organizer (see Chapter 12), a matrix (see Chapter 13), or a web to organize their information.

METACOGNITIVE DISCUSSION

Ask students to continue the log entry by identifying, in writing, one way in which the activity helped them better understand the function of one of the major organs and how the systems fit together. Have students share their log entries with members of their groups.

CLOSURE AND ASSESSMENT

Closure: Display completed graphics in the classroom. Celebrate the success of the activity with a round of applause or another type of celebration of your choice.

Assessment: Ask students to explain how the functioning of each of the systems would change if one of the organs were to be removed. Assign a specific "missing" organ to each small group. After groups have had an opportunity to discuss their answers, call on groups, selected at random, to share their answers with the rest of the class.

Have individual students complete a writing assignment in which they speculate on which of the organs in the digestive system they think would be the easiest to do without. Tell them that they need to supply supporting evidence for their predictions. Use a rubric to assess the quality of these individual essays. If your school does not have a rubric for scoring writing samples, you can quickly create one at http://rubistar.4teachers.org/index.php.

Have individual students use a matrix to organize information about the organs in the digestive and excretory systems. They will need to include information about the function of each organ, its positioning in the system, its size, its interaction with the rest of the system, and symptoms that indicate the organ is not functioning properly. A sample matrix is shown below.

Organ	Function	Position in system	Size and shape	Interaction with system	Symptoms

16

An Individual Writing Activity

Dear Uncle Chester

BACKGROUND

When students can explain a concept or phenomenon clearly in their own words, they demonstrate their personal ownership of the item. Asking students to write their explanations encourages them to focus their thoughts in order to express them as clearly as possible. Their successful completion of the writing assignment demonstrates basic understanding of the concept.

STANDARDS

This activity aligns with Science as Inquiry Standard 1: abilities necessary to do scientific inquiry and Unifying Concepts and Processes Standard 2: evidence, models, and explanation. In this activity, students communicate the procedure and results for an in-class activity, and they explain their observations in writing.

THINKING SKILL

Explaining, Applying, Generalizing

FOCUS ACTIVITY

Assign students to pairs. One member of each pair is the observer and the other is the recorder. Give each pair a small, clear glass and a hard-shell candy like an

M & M. Tell students to half-fill the small glass with water, drop in the M & M, and observe what happens for 5 minutes.

At the end of the observation period, call on pairs for their observations. Make a list of all of the different observations on the blackboard, overhead projector, chart paper, or an interactive whiteboard.

OBJECTIVE

To clearly explain a procedure and observations, and to speculate on the underlying causes of observed behaviors.

INPUT

Describe the importance of good explanations to the students. Do a think-pair-share. Ask students to think of a time when a poor explanation led them to an incorrect conclusion. Call on students at random to share their partners' examples of poor explanations with the class.

ACTIVITY

1. This is an individual writing activity.

2. Give each student a copy of the following paragraph. Have each student read the paragraph silently.

> Your assignment is to write a letter to your Uncle Chester in which you explain (*any concept or lab activity that the class has studied or done recently—this is an effective alternative to the traditional lab report*). Uncle Chester is very bright, but his formal education ended when he graduated from high school. He is very interested in you and what you are doing in school. He especially likes to hear about what you have learned or done recently in science class. Remember that you are explaining and speculating on causes for what you observed, so write the letter in your own words. Your goal is to help Uncle Chester understand (*the concept or lab activity*) just as well as he would if he were a member of this class. Make the letter as long as you think it needs to be so Uncle Chester knows what is going on. (Paper lengths will vary due to students' handwriting.)

3. Tell students that they are to write about the M & M activity.

4. Tell students that the rough drafts of the letters are due the following day.

5. The next day divide students into groups of three.

6. Tell students that they are going to proofread and critique each other's letters.

7. Tell them that after they have formed their circles, each student is to pass his or her letter to the student on his or her right.

8. That student is to read the letter, mark spelling and punctuation errors, and write marginal notes at points where they do not understand what is being said or believe that more needs to be said.

9. Proofreaders will have ten minutes to read the letters and critique them.

10. The original proofreader will pass the letter to the student on his or her right. The new proofreader will have five minutes to make additional comments. The second proofreader is really backing up the work done by the first.

11. The second proofreader will return the letter to its author. Each student will write a second draft of the letter as homework for the following day. The new draft is to address the corrections and other comments made by the proofreaders.

12. Tell students that you will collect and grade the second draft of the letter.

13. Return graded letters to students as quickly as possible.

COGNITIVE DISCUSSION

Do a think-pair-share. Ask students what they learned about dissolving and diffusion which are the processes by which the candy shell disappeared and its color spread through the water. Call on pairs to share their answers. Record the answers.

METACOGNITIVE DISCUSSION

Ask students what they found easiest about writing the letter. Ask them what was hardest about the writing. Ask if any of the students used a graphic organizer, such as a web, fishbone, mind map (see Chapter 20), or outline as a prewriting tool. Call on students at random to share their answers with the class. Ask students if they visualized Uncle Chester as they wrote to him. Brainstorm a picture of Uncle Chester.

CLOSURE AND ASSESSMENT

While students are working on their letters, write one general reply from Uncle Chester. Score the letters using a rubric (see Chapter 15 for help with rubrics). When graded letters are returned, read Uncle Chester's reply to the class.

17

A Jigsaw

Elements, Compounds, and Mixtures

BACKGROUND

Jigsaw is a way of dividing responsibility for teaching and learning among members of a group. Each member of the group is assigned a specific portion of the material to master. That person then may join other experts on the same portion of the material to decide how to teach the material and to practice those teaching strategies. Members of a team then rejoin each other for the actual teaching/learning. Jigsaw is most effective if this initial round of teaching and learning is followed by additional review of the material.

STANDARDS

This activity aligns with Unifying Concepts and Processes Standard 1: systems, order, and organization, and with Unifying Concepts and Processes Standard 2: evidence, models, and explanation. Students explore the classification of samples of matter as elements, compounds, or mixtures, evaluate the criteria that are used for classifying a given sample of matter, and teach each other.

THINKING SKILLS

Explaining (Teaching), Generalizing, Evaluating

FOCUS ACTIVITY

Do a think-pair-share. Ask students to tell you: (a) what famous detective is often (mis)quoted saying, "It is elementary, my dear Watson!"; (b) what you call a bone that is broken in more than one place; and (c) what you call the contents of a package that contains all of the ingredients that are needed to make a cake (except, perhaps, the liquid or eggs or shortening). Record the answer to each question on the board before proceeding to the next question.

OBJECTIVE

To be able to classify something as an element, a compound, or a mixture given its name or a description of one or more of its properties.

INPUT

Give each student a 3″ x 5″ card that has element, compound, or mixture written on it. Then ask students to pick up the passages that correspond to their cards (see pages 101–103 for blackline masters). Give them these passages at the end of class on the first day of the lesson and ask them to read their passages and be ready to discuss them with other experts on the same passage the next day.

> **ELEMENT:** Elements are pure substances that contain only one kind of atom. Two or more of these atoms may bond together to form molecules. Elements are the simplest substances known. Only about one hundred of them have been found in nature on earth. Elements cannot be chemically changed into other substances. Elements are homogeneous—all parts of an element look and act like all other parts of the same element. Some common elements are oxygen, hydrogen, copper, iron, gold, aluminum, and carbon.

> **COMPOUND:** Compounds are pure substances whose molecules are always identical. Atoms of two or more elements bond together to make molecules of compounds. Water molecules, for example, always contain two hydrogen atoms bonded to one oxygen atom. Silica molecules always contain one silicon atom bonded to two oxygen atoms. In a molecule of table salt, one sodium atom is bonded to one chlorine atom to produce sodium chloride. Compounds can be chemically broken apart into the elements that formed them. Compounds are homogeneous—all parts of a compound look and act like all other parts of the same compound. Millions of compounds are known. Some common compounds are salt, sugar, water, carbon dioxide, baking soda, and sulfuric acid.

> **MIXTURE:** Mixtures contain two or more elements or compounds that are not chemically combined. The composition of a mixture may vary—there are lots of different ways to make salt water, for example. The percents of the two substances in the mixture will not always be the same. Mixtures may be separated physically or chemically. To separate a salt water mixture, you could just let the water evaporate out of the mixture. Mixtures are not always this easy to separate. It may be very tricky to separate a mixture of salt and sugar. Mixtures may
>
> *(Continued)*

(Continued)

be homogeneous—all parts of the mixture may look and act the same. Milk and mayonnaise are homogeneous mixtures. Mixtures may also be heterogeneous—different parts of the mixture may look and act differently. Asphalt and wood are heterogeneous mixtures. Millions of mixtures are known. There are more natural mixtures than elements or compounds. Some common mixtures are milk, wood, vinegar, concrete, brick, dirt, dishwater, and a pail of garbage.

ACTIVITY

1. Hand out the element, compound, and mixture cards and have students pick up the reading passages toward the end of class. Tell students to read their individual passages before the next class meeting.

2. At the beginning of the next class period, get expert groups together. Form groups of three. This means that you will have three or four groups for each category. Have each expert group plan a teaching strategy and have each expert in each group do a graphic that he or she will use as part of the teaching process. Check out progress and understanding in the expert groups. It is vital that you, the teacher, monitor the expert groups to correct misunderstandings before the teaching round begins. When an expert group finishes its work, tell members to thank each other and return to their seats to wait for further instructions.

3. You may want to place a time limit of ten minutes on the expert group portion of this lesson. This will encourage students to stay on task and to get the job done in a reasonable amount of time.

4. When all expert groups are finished, divide the class into groups of three. Each group is to contain one student from element, one from compound, and one from mixture.

5. Have each expert teach his or her portion of the material to the rest of the group. Tell students that their job as learners is to listen actively, ask questions, and request clarification of ideas that they do not understand. Their job as teachers is to explain their portion of the material, using the visual they created as a teaching tool, and to answer questions and clarify information for the members of their group.

6. Have students do the next round—teaching and learning in turn. Again it is vital that you, the teacher, monitor the groups and correct any misunderstandings that you observe.

7. Encourage students to thank each other at the end of this round.

COGNITIVE DISCUSSION

Have students write a log entry in which they record the best, most complete definitions of element, compound, and mixture that they can recall without referring to the visual or the reading.

METACOGNITIVE DISCUSSION

Ask students to think and jot down individual answers to be shared with their groups:

1. Which was harder, teaching or listening?
2. What was the most effective teaching strategy used by a member of the group?
3. How could the teaching strategies be improved?
4. Did you take any notes when you were a listener?
5. Does taking notes help you as a learner?

CLOSURE AND ASSESSMENT

Closure: Call on students at random to contribute ideas from their cognitive log entries to make a class summary of elements, compounds, and mixtures. Record their answers in an outline or a mind map on the blackboard, chart paper, or an interactive whiteboard. Fill in any glaring omissions. Thank students for a job well done.

Assessment: Give each student a matrix (see Chapter 13 and the following example) in which you have listed appearance, components, and behavior of several samples of matter, and direct them to classify each sample as an element, compound, or mixture. Check the accuracy of their classifications.

Sample	Appearance	Components	Behavior
1	Tiny grains, all the same size and color, all shiny	Dextrose	Entire sample dissolves when added to water
2	Tiny grains, all the same size and color, all shiny	Dextrose and sodium chloride	Entire sample dissolves when added to water
3	Tiny grains, different sizes and colors	Silica, sodium chloride, and magnetite	Some of the sample does not dissolve in water
4	Two layers of liquid, one green and one blue	Oil, water, and dye	Layers mix when container is shaken and separate upon standing
5	Reddish powder	Copper	Does not dissolve in water, is not attracted to a magnet

Tell individual students to write a paragraph in which they tell, in general, tests that they might perform to tell whether a sample is a pure substance or a mixture. Score the paragraphs using a rubric.

18

Follow-Up for Guided Practice

Elements, Compounds, and Mixtures

BACKGROUND

Although proponents of cooperative learning view jigsaw as an excellent way to promote interdependence among members of a group, critics insist that jigsaw can be one of the least effective ways for students to learn new information or concepts. The critics may be correct if teachers who use a jigsaw overlook one key component of all learning—follow-up of initial activities with guided practice and drill.

STANDARDS

This activity aligns with Unifying Concepts and Processes Standard 1: systems, order, and organization, and with Science as Inquiry Standard 1: abilities necessary to do scientific inquiry. Students apply the definitions they learned in Chapter 17 to new examples and demonstrate their understanding of the categories of matter.

THINKING SKILLS

Identifying Ideas, Analyzing, Applying

FOCUS ACTIVITY

The initial jigsaw provides the focus activity for the follow-up.

OBJECTIVES

To be able to apply the definitions of elements, compounds, and mixtures to new examples; to use previously learned information in a new activity.

INPUT

Give each student a copy of the follow-up activity. Rotate the focus. The student who initially learned and taught information about elements is to look for compounds in the follow-up. The student who initially dealt with compounds is to focus on mixtures. The mixtures student is to look for elements. Assign initial work on the follow-up as homework.

ACTIVITY

1. Hand out the follow-up activity worksheet. Be sure that students understand that the focus is to rotate—and how to rotate. Be sure that each student knows what to look for as he or she does the follow-up as homework. You may use household items like buttons, nuts, bolts, and washers to create hands-on manipulatives to use in place of pictures 4, 5, 6, 13, 14, and 15.

2. Before groups begin the next day, tell them that each person is to tell the group which items in the follow-up activity belong to his or her category and why that item fits the category. If members of a group disagree about how to classify an item, they must discuss their reasons for wanting to classify it in different ways and reach consensus about the best way to categorize or classify the item before they move on to another.

3. When the group has finished classifying the items on the follow-up, they are to sign one completed copy of the follow-up sheet and turn it in. Their signatures signify that they all agree to accept the grade earned by the paper that is turned in.

4. Call on a student to repeat the instructions.

5. Have groups circle and complete the activity.

COGNITIVE DISCUSSION

After all groups have turned in their papers, go over the answers for the follow-up. Have a copy of the activity on the overhead. Call on groups at random to tell how they classified an item and why they so classified it. Discuss the answers, especially if there is disagreement (from you or another group) with the initial answer. Be sure that the class knows the right answers and why those answers are correct before they leave the room.

Elements, Compounds, and Mixtures

Applying What We Have Learned

Directions: Decide which of the following is an example of _____.

(an element, a compound, or a mixture)

Circle your choices (answers).

1. copper	2. air	3. distilled water
4.	5.	6.
7. contains two or more kinds of atoms always present in the same ratio(s)	8. contains a single kind of atom or molecule	9. contains two or more kinds of atoms or molecules
10. contains a single kind of atom	11. may be heterogeneous	12. must be homogeneous
13.	14.	15.

METACOGNITIVE DISCUSSION

Have students write a log entry in which they compare and contrast the attributes of elements, compounds, and mixtures. Emphasize that they are developing a general description of each category. Tell them that they may use a graphic organizer, such as a three-way Venn diagram, a fishbone, or a mind map in place of descriptive paragraphs. Students will rely on their memories as they write. Have them continue the log entry by writing one unanswered question that they still have about the topic.

CLOSURE AND ASSESSMENT

Closure: Call on students at random to share their questions with the class. Make a list of the questions on the overhead, chart paper, or the interactive whiteboard. Save the questions and refer to them as you progress with your study of the topic. Ask students to answer their own questions when class activities have provided them with the information that they need to develop those answers.

Assessment: On an ongoing basis, check each student's identification of samples of materials that are used in various lab activities. Ask students to use labels from consumer products to classify those goods as elements, compounds, or mixtures.

Give pairs of students sandwich bags filled with a variety of small objects such as buttons, hooks, eyes, Velcro hooks of varied colors, Velcro eyes of varied colors, nuts, and bolts and tell pairs that their task is to use the objects to create a variety of representations of elements, compounds, and mixtures. Check the accuracy of their representations.

19

Using a Storyboard

Home on the Range Just Is Not the Same

BACKGROUND

Good thinkers are skilled in visualizing and predicting. The more clearly one can see, the better one can understand a problem or situation. It was Leo Szilard's ability to see a neutron penetrating and splitting a nucleus that led to the successful splitting of the atom. His visualization of the process not only enabled him to convince others that splitting the atom was possible, but allowed scientists to predict which kinds of atoms should be easiest to split. The more skilled students become at visualizing and predicting, the more effectively they will think.

STANDARDS

This activity aligns with Unifying Concepts and Processes Standard 4: evolution and equilibrium. As they work through the activity, students need to brainstorm ways in which large animals, dinosaurs, might have evolved if they had survived to the present day and to predict the ways in which their survival would have affected the ecosystems to which they belong.

THINKING SKILLS

Visualizing, Predicting, Imagining, Speculating, Hypothesizing

FOCUS ACTIVITY

Ask students to close their eyes and picture themselves getting ready for school. Tell them to see the scene in as much detail as possible. Have each student share his or her visualization with a partner.

OBJECTIVE

To practice the skills of visualizing and predicting.

INPUT

Give students a copy of the following scenario or show it on the overhead projector or interactive whiteboard (see page 104 for a reproducible master).

> Clint Cody is a modern-day cattle rancher in southern Wyoming. He runs his cattle on several thousand acres of grassland and forest. Clint loves ranching, except for one problem. It is really hard dealing with issues caused by several kinds of dinosaurs. You see, dinosaurs never became extinct. Clint must deal with dinosaur-related situations each day.
>
> Draw a storyboard that shows one day in Clint's life.

Tell students that a storyboard is like a comic strip. It tells a story in a series of pictures. The pictures may be accompanied by text. Storyboards are used to plan television commercials and programs, to plot movies, and to design and describe complex tasks in a variety of settings.

ACTIVITY

1. Assign a rough draft of the storyboard as homework. Tell students that a good storyboard has more pictures than text, uses color lavishly, and may be funny.

2. The next day divide the class into groups of three.

3. Each group is to do a storyboard on a large sheet of paper.

4. Remind students to use the DOVE guidelines as they brainstorm their group stories.

5. Ask for questions. Then have groups do their storyboards.

COGNITIVE DISCUSSION

Have students write a log entry in which they discuss all of the facts about dinosaurs that they needed to recall in doing their stories. Tell them to include a description of any use of graphic organizers as prewriting tools. Call on students at random to list responses.

METACOGNITIVE DISCUSSION

Have groups discuss how they resolved differences in individual stories to obtain the group story, what they feel they did well in producing the storyboard, and what they would do differently if they were to do it over.

Have each student do a log entry discussing the process of visualizing a hypothesis. Ask students to write in some detail about how they approached the assignment. Ask them to reconstruct their thinking step by step.

CLOSURE AND ASSESSMENT

Closure: Have each group present its storyboard to the class. Display the storyboards in the classroom.

Assessment: Have individual students outline, map (see Chapter 20), or storyboard the "aha"s that they experienced about the effect of adding a large animal to an ecosystem on the evolution of that system. Tell them to include information explaining the difference between a major predator and a prey species on the evolution of the system. Score each student's product using a rubric whose criteria include clear understanding of relationships among species and the roles of predators and prey on an ecosystem.

20
Mapping
Making Sense of What We Know

BACKGROUND

A mind map is a diagram that is used to organize information and show relationships that exist between different pieces of the information. Maps can be used in place of outlines. Maps are particularly appealing to nonlinear thinkers.

STANDARDS

This activity aligns with Unifying Concepts and Processes Standard 1: systems, order, and organization, and with Science as Inquiry Standard 1: abilities necessary to do scientific inquiry. As they do this activity, students will learn how they can use mind mapping to organize, summarize, and symbolize information.

THINKING SKILLS

Analyzing, Summarizing, Visualizing, Symbolizing, Relating

FOCUS ACTIVITY

Review the scientific inquiry process, focusing on key inquiry elements such as careful observation, formulating questions, brainstorming hypotheses, testing hypotheses, recognizing alternatives, and drawing reasonable conclusions.

OBJECTIVE

To organize and analyze information.

INPUT

Teach students the rules for mapping. It is particularly effective to map the rules on the board, overhead, or chart paper rather than just listing them. For online examples, do a search for "Tony Buzan," or go to http://www.peterrussell.com/MindMaps/HowTo.php.

RULES FOR MAPPING

1. Do maps on plain white paper.

2. Start maps at the center of the paper. The title and a picture illustrating the title are in the center, not at the top of the paper.

3. Print all text using both upper and lower case letters. Follow standard conventions for use of cases.

4. Use a thick line leading from the center (title) to carry each main idea. Use thin lines hanging or branching from the thick ones to carry supporting details.

5. Use one color for lines and text for each main idea and its details. Use a different color for each main idea.

6. Use pictures to illustrate text. Try to minimize words and maximize use of pictures or graphics. Think of the mind map as a captioned photo album.

7. Delete incorrect information by crossing it out.

8. Think outside the paper. Add more paper to the original piece as needed to extend the mind map.

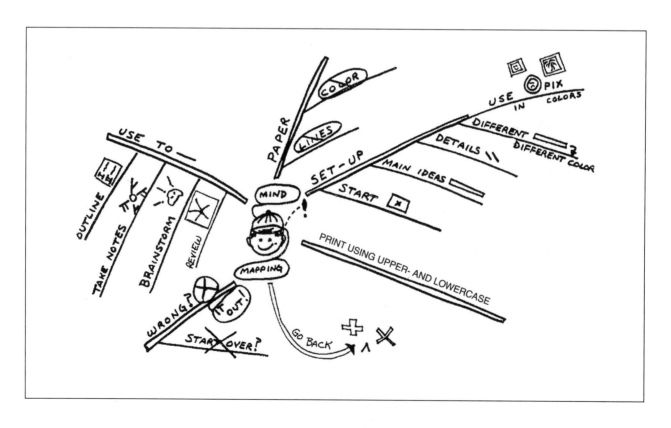

ACTIVITY

1. Place a large, transparent container that is about two-thirds filled with water on your desk. The container needs to be large enough to hold 4 cans of carbonated soda pop with room to spare, and it needs to be at least twice as tall as an individual pop can.

2. Hold up a can of regular pop and one of diet pop of the same brand, and tell students to write a list of any differences they notice about the two cans of pop in their daily log entry.

3. Place the can of regular pop in the container of water and let go of the can. It will sink to the bottom of the container.

4. Place the can of diet pop in the container of water and let go of the can. It will float.

5. Assign students to small groups of three. Each group needs to have a conductor who keeps the group on time and on task and presents the mind map to the rest of the class, an illustrator who sketches the mind-map visuals, and a correspondent who draws the lines and does the writing.

6. Tell students that the task is to brainstorm reasons why the regular pop sinks and the diet pop floats. Suggest that they may want to include information describing what they know about the two kinds of pop. Say that they need to include ideas about testing their hypotheses.

7. Say that the correspondent may come to the desk to inspect the cans of pop and write down information about the two kinds of pop.

8. Check for understanding of the instructions. Ask randomly selected students to describe the task for the class.

9. Give the small groups time to brainstorm and complete their mind maps. Older students can complete the map in about 15 minutes. Younger students may need varying amounts of time.

There is a sample map summarizing information about copper at the end of this chapter (see page 75). Students may find a sample helpful as they structure their own mind maps.

COGNITIVE DISCUSSION

Call on groups at random to present their maps to the rest of the class. Ask each group what members want to do to test their hypotheses about why the regular pop sinks and the diet pop floats. List the ideas on the board, chart paper, the overhead projector or an interactive whiteboard.

You may or may not want to have students test their hypotheses right away. They will need some extra materials, such as balance scales, small empty containers, and sugar to do the testing.

METACOGNITIVE DISCUSSION

Ask students to write a log entry in which they identify the following:

One way that I can use mapping in another class is . . .

One good idea that I got from another student's map is . . .

One way that I will improve my mapping technique the next time is . . .

CLOSURE AND ASSESSMENT

Closure: Display the group or individual maps in the classroom.

Assessment: Have individual students map their thoughts about the scientific inquiry process. As you score individual maps, look for key inquiry elements such as careful observation, formulating questions, brainstorming hypotheses, testing hypotheses, recognizing alternatives, and drawing reasonable conclusions.

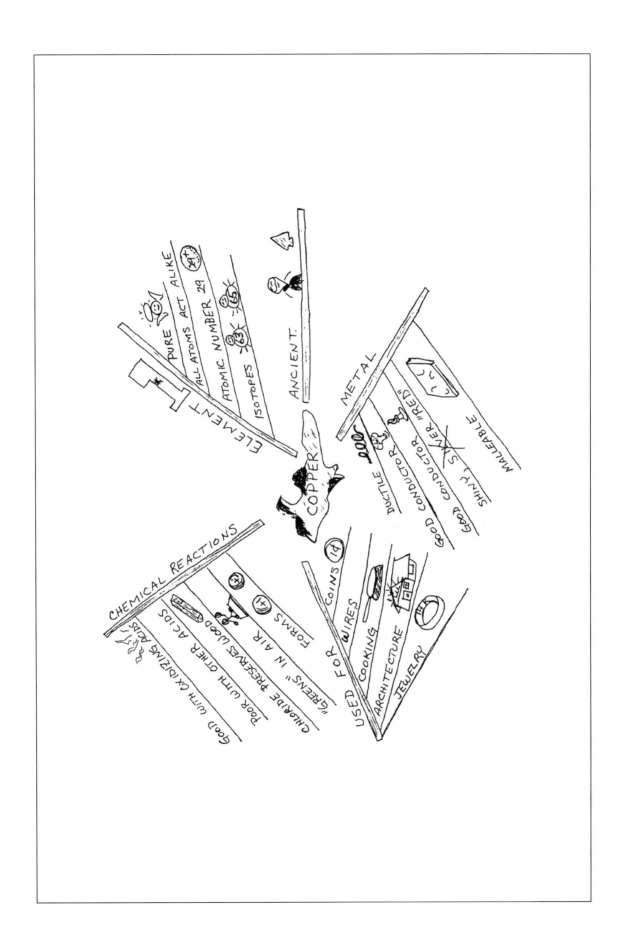

75

21

Right-Angle Thinking

Molecules in Motion

BACKGROUND

Right-angle thinking forces students to associate ideas and to generalize or draw conclusions based on acquired information. Using the graphic organizer helps them see their thinking in action.

STANDARDS

This activity aligns with Unifying Concepts and Processes Standard 1: systems, order, and organization, and with Science as Inquiry Standard 1: abilities necessary to do scientific inquiry. In the course of this activity, students develop deeper understanding of the molecular differences that exist among the states of matter, how those differences can be used to explain the behaviors of the physical states, and the importance of careful observation and modeling.

THINKING SKILLS

Associating Ideas, Drawing Conclusions, Evaluating, Generalizing

FOCUS ACTIVITY

Do the following demonstration: place a small volume of sand in one balloon, a small volume of water in a second, and a small volume of air in a third. Ask students to jot down a few notes about the behavior of each balloon. Next, pour a small volume of sand into the center of a large (one liter) beaker, a small volume of water in the center of a second beaker, and a small volume of air into the center of a third. Ask students to jot down a few notes about the behavior of each sample of matter. Finally, fill one large syringe (without the needle!) with sand, fill a second with water, and a third with air. Push on the plunger of each syringe after filling it—try to compress each sample. Ask students to jot down a few notes about the compressibility of each sample.

OBJECTIVE

To use right-angle thinking to associate compressibility and shape of solids, liquids, and gases with motion of molecules and distances between molecules.

INPUT

Discuss the notes that students wrote during the observation. Call on students at random to share their observations with the rest of the class (ask each student who is called on to share one specific observation). Use these observations to guide students to the following ideas: solids are not compressible and do not rely on their containers for their shapes; liquids are not compressible but do rely on their containers for their shapes; gases are very compressible and rely on their containers for their shapes.

ACTIVITY

1. Divide students into groups of three.

2. Tell students that their task is to complete a right-angle thinking diagram (see figure on page 78) for each of the states of matter: solid, liquid, and gas.

3. The horizontal arm of each diagram is used to describe shape-dependence and compressibility of one of the states of matter.

4. The vertical arm of the diagram is used to describe distances between molecules, their freedom (or lack of it) to move from place to place in that state of matter, and other possible types of molecular motion.

5. Each member of the group is to complete one of the three diagrams and explain his or her conclusions about molecular motion and spacing to the other members of the group.

6. Ask for questions. Call on a student selected at random to repeat the instructions.

7. Set a time limit for the activity.

8. Ask each group to have a scout pick up three copies of the right-angle thinking diagram.

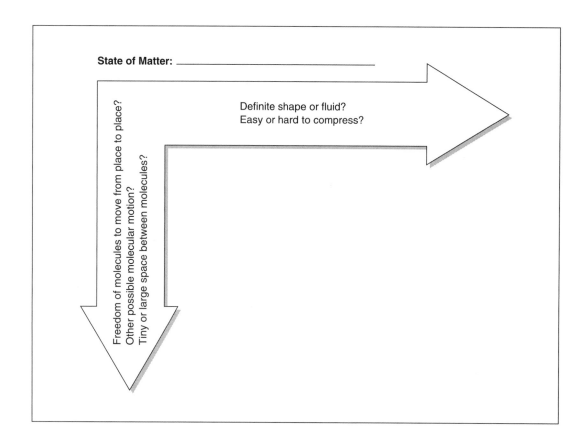

COGNITIVE DISCUSSION

Check the right-angle diagrams for correctness as groups work. Then have each student recreate the two diagrams taught by groupmates from memory (as much as possible). The member of the group who did the original diagram will supervise as the others complete the new diagrams. The supervisor may help his or her groupmates complete their diagrams, but may not simply give them his or her diagram to copy.

METACOGNITIVE DISCUSSION

Have students complete the following log entry:

I am *most* like a molecule in a (*name the physical state*) because (*describe personal motion and closeness to others*) . . .

I am *least* like a molecule in a (*name the physical state*) because (*give reasons related to motion and closeness to others*) . . .

What I learned about associating ideas is . . .

How I developed my right-angle was . . . (*back and forth between horizontal and vertical arms? Complete one arm and then do the other? Stop to think and generate ideas? Look for alternatives?*)

CLOSURE AND ASSESSMENT

Closure: Divide the class into three groups of approximately equal size. Give each group a physical state to role play and a few moments to plan their actions. Then have groups do the role playing. Finish with a round of applause.

Assessment: Tell students to return to their groups of three. Have each group do a storyboard in which they show the changes that occur on the molecular level as a solid melts and a liquid evaporates. Tell groups to focus on both the gradual changes in molecular motion that occur as the temperature rises and the rapid changes that occur during melting and evaporation. Score the storyboards for accuracy and completeness using a rubric.

PART IV

Designing Your Own Activities

22

Designing Your Own Activities

Your Turn!

N|ow that you've had an opportunity to review the activities in this book and, perhaps, try a few with your students, you are probably asking: "How do I move on? How do I design more lessons that I can use in my classroom with my students? How can lessons like these work with my curriculum?"

Designing your own activities will take some practice and planning, and the more you do, the easier the task will become. I believe that the best place to start is with your own science materials. Here are some pointers that you can use to infuse thinking skills into your lessons.

THE ACTIVITY MODEL

You have probably noticed that each of the activities in this book follows the same model or lesson design. The elements in this lesson model deepen your thinking about lesson planning so that your lessons lead to better student thinking (Andrade, 1999). A reproducible master at the end of this book gives you the lesson template (see page 106). I encourage you to make your lesson plans part of your personal log so that your plans and reflections are combined in one resource that you can use for designing even better lessons next time.

Some sections of the lesson model may take less time to develop than others. Your science text or curriculum materials may already identify the national standards with which lessons align, individual lesson objectives, and step-by-step instructions for doing the lesson including a Focus Activity, Input, the Activity itself, and Closure. You may need to spend more time mulling over the Background, which connects the lesson to prior and future knowledge, the Thinking Skills (more on this later), the

Cognitive and Metacognitive Discussions, and ideas for Assessment. My advice is that you use every step in the template to design the richest, most complete, most thoughtful lessons possible.

METACOGNITION: A KEY INGREDIENT

The lesson model used in this book is very metacognitive. When many people hear *metacognition,* they think "reflection and self-evaluation," but this is only one of the metacognitive processes. For learning to be most effective, these valuable cognitive processes need to be incorporated into planning an activity, monitoring progress during the activity, and reflecting and evaluating at the conclusion of the activity.

When you engage in metacognition to develop a lesson plan, lead students through the lesson, and process and reflect, you will do the following:

PLANNING

- Build on what you already know to develop new insights (Background).
- Define the goal of the lesson (Standards, Thinking Skills, and Objective).
- Organize the steps that are necessary to complete the task (Focus Activity, Input, Activity, Closure).

MONITORING

- Lead students through the lesson (Activity).
- Monitor small groups for progress toward the overall goal (Activity).
- Intervene in the group process as needed (Activity).
- Take time out to revise directions or add new ones (Activity).

EVALUATING

- Identify and discuss the learning (Cognitive Discussion).
- Reflect on the learning progress (Metacognitive Discussion).
- Assess student learning (Assessment).

If you follow this lesson model, you will find yourself taking greater charge of your lesson planning and becoming more aware of the effectiveness of your planning as you monitor and evaluate how well your lessons work in the classroom. You may find yourself using metacognitive planning more and more often, in and out of the classroom. You may find yourself carrying on an internal dialogue, asking yourself:

- Where are we in this lesson?
- Is the lesson taking students where I want them to go?
- Do I need to stop the activity and give revised instructions?
- Which students or groups seem to be doing well?
- Which students or groups seem to need extra attention?
- Are students finishing faster than expected?
- Will students need extra time?

After finishing an activity, as you note observations in your log, you may also ask and answer questions like these:

- What results did I want from this lesson?
- How well did the lesson work?
- What specifically worked well?
- How might I improve it next time?
- Do I want any help in improving the lesson? Who might help me?

The metacognitive discussion built into each activity is there to help students develop their own abilities to monitor progress toward a goal and self-evaluate. Students who develop metacognitive skills become more successful, confident, independent learners (Halter, n.d.), and it is important to remember that metacognition does not come automatically. I once heard a speaker say that people who are not good at metacognition are doomed to go through life repeating the same mistakes over and over and over again because they do not know why they are making the mistakes. They have never learned to self-monitor and self-evaluate.

One of the most powerful ways that you can help students improve this key skill is to think out loud as you lead a lesson and tell them what you are doing and why you are doing it when you do it. Instead of silently thinking, "Where are we in this lesson?" ask the question out loud and then say, "I thought I'd better do some monitoring of our progress." When you sense that a lesson is not going in the desired direction, or when you realize that you forgot to give an important piece of information or direction, make a noise like the back-up beeper on a piece of heavy machinery, "BEEP, BEEP, BEEP!" and tell students, "That was my back-up beeper telling me that I need to tell you . . ." Remember, I taught high school students, and they loved my back-up beeper. When I run into some of my former students at events at my "old" high school, they often tell me that they still use the back-up beeper signal to self-correct during their daily activities.

Thinking out loud continues at the end of a lesson. Model for students your own self-evaluation of the lesson. Do it as an analogy if you wish: "For me, this lesson was like doing a load of laundry because most of the activity came out 'clean' and led to the results I hoped for, but a few of the steps need additional attention, just like some pieces of laundry need extra spot removers, and there seemed to be a missing step close to the beginning, just like that sock that never makes it in with the rest of the load." Or you can do your self-evaluation of the lesson straight: "When I planned this activity, I wanted certain results (*go into detail if you wish*). The following steps worked well (*follow with specifics*). I'll have students do other steps differently next time (*add the details*). Maybe you can help me by telling me where you felt you needed better or different procedures or instructions to follow."

Take time to reflect; make time to reflect. Metacognition is one of the most precious skills you can give your students.

SELECTING AN ACTIVITY

Enough background, you may be thinking. How do I actually get started? Begin by selecting an activity. Look through the science activities that you will have students do in the upcoming few weeks, ask colleagues for suggestions, comb through references that contain large numbers of suggestions for activities. There are some excellent resources available online; a Web search for "hands-on science activities" or "inquiry-based science activities" will produce scores of sources to investigate. I am thinking that, given the demands on classroom teachers to "cover the curriculum" or "get ready for the (state) test," you will probably be happiest if you select an activity that is already in your course or grade-level syllabus. *(Did you recognize the metacognition?)*

Look at the activity closely. In the teachers' materials that accompany many recently published textbooks and curriculum packages, you will probably find much of the material that you want to include in your plan. As noted earlier in this chapter, these sources often indicate alignment with national science standards and curriculum objectives, and they also may include detailed instructions for activities. The Focus Activity, Input, Activity, and Closure may be done for you already. If they are, this is a good time for metacognition! As you read through the instructions, ask yourself if they sound complete or if you think that some expansion or modification is needed. If the instructions include a hands-on activity, it is always a good idea to do a trial run to be sure that the activity works as described. Disaster can strike hard and fast when you do untested hands-on activities with students.

THE THREE-STORY INTELLECT

Now you want to align that activity with at least one targeted thinking skill. As you read through the activity, frequently look through the Three-Story Intellect diagram in the beginning of this book (page xii) and ask yourself which thinking skills, listed inside and to the right of the house in the diagram, seem to align with the activity. Will students be *gathering* information by asking questions, reading, doing a hands-on activity, watching a video, or engaging in some other task? Will they be *processing* information, clarifying and crystallizing their understanding of information that they have gathered? Will they be *applying* their learning, branching out to new applications, finding new meaning, creating visualizations, predicting consequences, or imagining alternatives? Every good activity aligns with standards and objectives, and every good activity also aligns with thinking skills. You may need to dig out the thinking skills, but they are there.

GRAPHIC ORGANIZERS

Some of the most powerful thinking tools in your toolbox are graphic organizers. These tools not only make thinking visible, they also pattern and organize information.

Making thinking visible can take many forms. For instance, the advice "Think out loud in front of your students" makes your thinking visible, because it reveals the processes that are occurring inside your head to your students.

Using sketches, diagrams, and other visuals as teaching or reporting tools is another way to make thinking visible. Perkins (2003) discusses leading students through a lesson by showing them a satellite photograph of a hurricane without any identifying information and asking them two questions: "What's going on here?" and "What do you see that supports your thinking?" The photograph showed the outline of the state of Florida through a classic hurricane spiral cloud formation complete with eye wall, and students quickly used those features of the photograph to decipher its meaning.

When I was teaching, I would often ask students to "tell me in words and show me in pictures" what was happening on the molecular level during some simple physical processes. Here's an example: when a gas is heated, it expands because the individual molecules, the model says, move faster and farther apart. The molecular size does not change. If students "showed" me molecules that were moving faster by drawing pictures of them being farther apart and more swollen than their cooler selves, with larger vectors or arrows to represent greater speed, I knew their understanding of what was happening was not completely accurate, and I would review the material with those students who needed to correct misunderstandings.

Graphic organizers not only make thinking visible, they also pattern information, and the human brain thrives on patterns (Caine, Caine, McClintic, & Klimek, 2005). Patterning describes how the brain organizes and categorizes information, and all decisions about where to focus, what to learn, what to remember and what to forget, and how to proceed are based on our personal patterns. We want information to make sense, and that means we want information to fit together in ways that make it useful to us. Graphic organizers, used judiciously and strategically, help students create the organization and categorization that the brain craves and to do it in a way that makes the learning conceptually and factually accurate. In other words, students not only "get" the content, they get it right. You have probably noticed, as you have worked your way through this book, that I use graphic organizers in a variety of ways. I use them as brainstorming or information-gathering tools; I employ them as analyzing, comparing, contrasting, linking, and distinguishing information-processing tools, and I use them as imagining, predicting, hypothesizing, concluding, and generalizing information-applying tools. I *love* graphic organizers.

Here are just a few words of advice. When you introduce students to a graphic organizer, have them use it during a fairly easy or fun task first. That way they can focus on the use of the tool rather than the content of the lesson. The dinosaur storyboard in Chapter 19, for example, is one that doesn't seem serious at first. It is only when students consider the implications of a large potential prey or predator animal not going extinct, how that animal may have evolved over the eons, and the effect its presence could have on an ecosystem that the "what if" behind the storyboard becomes less whimsical.

Do not introduce too many graphic organizers too fast. Give students a chance to use a graphic organizer several times before introducing a new one. I had some definite favorites that I used over and over and over again, and students did not get tired of using them. My favorites included the two- and three-way Venn diagrams, the right angle, the fishbone, the storyboard, and the Tony Buzan mind map. (I use mind mapping quite often; it's the tool I used to brainstorm this chapter.) If you are not familiar with graphic organizers and effective ways to use them, you can find many excellent resources online, and I highly recommend Jim Bellanca's *A Guide to Graphic Organizers* (2007) as a smorgasbord of graphic organizer choices and uses.

THINKING OUTSIDE THE ROWS

Using cooperative learning groups and tapping into all of your students' multiple intelligences will encourage student engagement in classroom activities and scaffold the development of higher-order thinking skills (Caine et al., 2005). All students are both similar to and different from each other; all students can learn to use metacognition to develop self-direction and a sense of self-efficacy, and they will learn more effectively when their own unique abilities and intelligences are engaged. Assigning students to cooperative groups and assigning group tasks that require the use of manipulatives, the performance of skits or songs, and the production of large graphics will encourage the feelings of relaxed alertness and empowerment that result in deeper learning.

The mentoring that students provide to each other in cooperative groups can also promote better thinking. Kluger (2007) notes that a study of the influence of birth order on personal development showed that first-born siblings typically score higher on a standard IQ test than their younger brothers and sisters. Although the reasons for this are not clear, many researchers believe that the mentoring of their younger siblings gives first-borns an intellectual boost that results in their higher IQ scores. In cooperative learning activities that are carefully structured and monitored, all students share the mentoring role, so all students grow better thinking skills.

Many of how-to books that describe successful implementation of cooperative learning stress these three guidelines:

1. Small groups work better than large ones. For most classroom tasks and activities, groups of two to four students work best. Large groups work well if the product is a skit or a song. The Closure activity in Chapter 21 in this book is a good example of this.

2. Teacher-assigned heterogeneous groups produce the best results. As mentioned in the Preface, teachers know how to partner students with learning difficulties or English language learners with students whose mentoring skills are strong. This results in better learning for all.

3. You need to coach students in effective use of teamwork skills and give them opportunities to practice those skills. Remember to leave groups together long enough for students to establish trust, which leads to positive interdependence and constructive working relationships. During Metacognitive Reflection, have groups process their use of teamwork skills and set goals for improvement.

If you are looking for help in implementing cooperative learning in your classroom, you will find several cooperative learning guidebooks listed in the Reference section of this book. Cooperative learning, if employed thoughtfully and well, can be one of a teacher's most valuable tools in helping all students meet learning goals. Much time and planning must be put into developing a thoughtful cooperative learning activity, and the payback can be enormous.

THE BIG PICTURE

It is time to put the pieces together. To plan your own activities, you will want to do the following:

1. Make a copy of the template. Whether you write on it or not, the lesson plan template is your planning tool and guide.

2. Get metacognitive. Remind yourself that it is going to take time and thought to work through the plan.

3. Select an activity. Look ahead in your curriculum and identify a simple activity to use. It is always best to start small and simple so that you can focus on the process rather than getting ensnared in the content.

4. Align the activity with the Three-Story Intellect. Find one or more thinking skills that the activity targets.

5. Tie in a graphic organizer. Remember that these powerful tools help the brain pattern the new information and connect it to prior learning.

6. Make up your cooperative learning groups. Remember to make them heterogeneous and to carefully place English language learners or students with special learning needs with strong mentors.

7. Do the activity. As students work in small groups, monitor their progress. Get metacognitive. Stop the activity to revise directions as needed; stop groups to correct misunderstandings as they arise.

8. Stay metacognitive. Reflect. In your log, note what worked well and what you want to do differently next time.

9. Have fun. Your playfulness will help students feel more relaxed and will contribute to the safe-risk climate that leads to better learning.

Follow the plan, model thinking for your students, and you will catch them, and yourself, becoming better thinkers in science and in everyday life.

Reproducibles

DOVE Guidelines

Defer judgment; anything goes

Opt for original; different ideas

Vast number is needed

Expand by piggybacking on others' ideas

Mrs. Potter's Questions

1. What were you supposed to do?

2. What did you do well?

3. What would you do differently next time?

4. Do you need any help?

People Search

Directions: Find someone who can give you an answer for each of the items below. A classmate may sign for only one item, so you will need ten different signatures. Sign only if you know the answer, or else be prepared to accept the consequences!

My signature means that I . . .

1. _____

_____

2. _____

_____

3. _____

_____

4. _____

_____

5. _____

_____

6. _____

_____

7. _____

_____

8. _____

_____

9. _____

_____

10. _____

_____

KNL		
K (What do we *Know*?)	**N** (What do we *Need* to know?)	**L** (What have we *Learned*?)

Asking Questions to Learn What I Want to Learn

Question Level	My Goal Is . . .	Some Key Words to Use Are . . .
Gathering Knowledge (First-Story Intellect)	to learn simple facts; to collect basic information	who, what, when, where, which, name, list, identify, define, how much, how many, measure, describe
Processing Knowledge (Second-Story Intellect)	to solve problems; to use knowledge in a different context or situation	compare, contrast, explain, solve, what else, instead (of), in addition to, why, my reasons are, next, in review, in conclusion, in summary, this means
Applying Knowledge (Third-Story Intellect)	to explain my opinions; to take a position; to justify an answer; to express new ideas	devise, design, develop, I predict, I believe, in my judgment, it is my opinion (that), it seems, what if

Prediction Guide: _____

Directions: Read each statement. Start with the "ME" column and place a "+" if you agree or a "0" if you disagree with the statement. Then read the textbook and decide whether or not the author agrees with the statement. Again use "+" or a "0." Change all "0" statements so they agree with the textbook, and write down the page number of where you found the information.

ME	AUTHOR	STATEMENTS

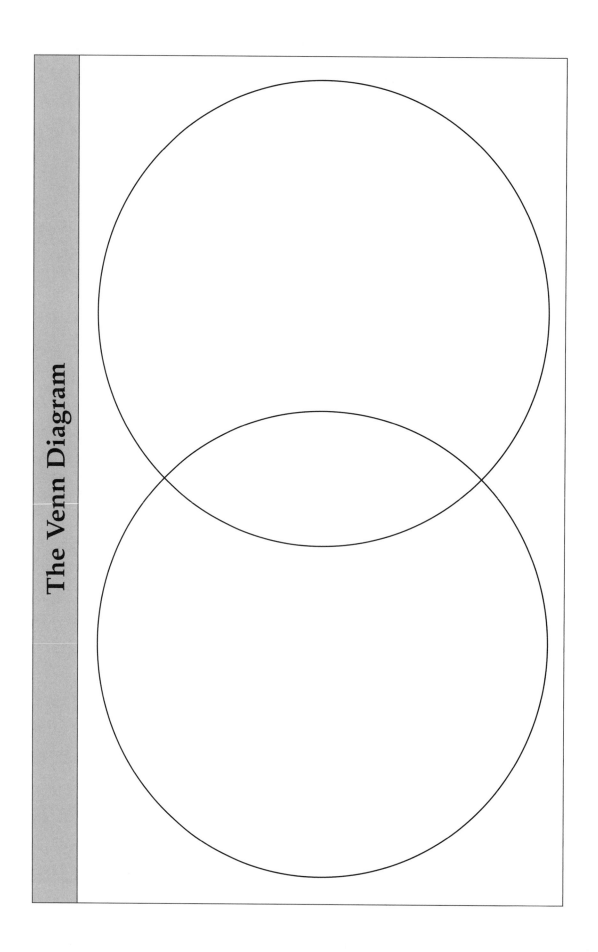

The Venn Diagram

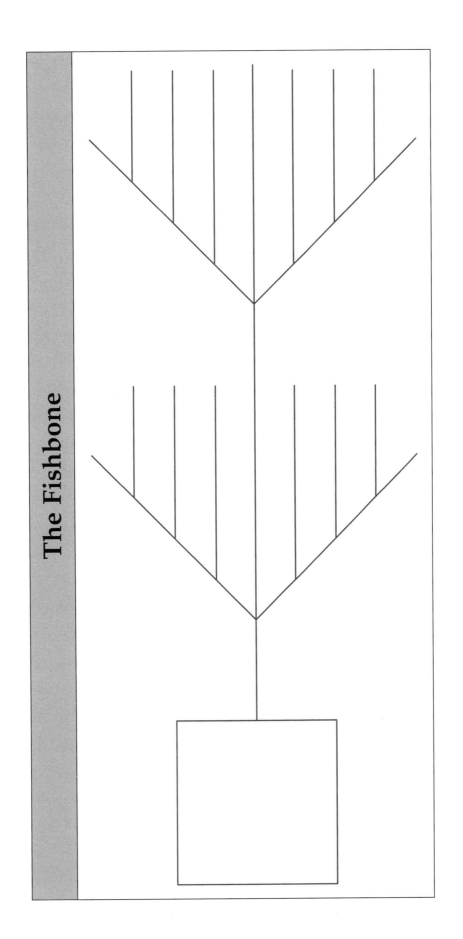

The Fishbone

A Checklist: Observed Use of Targeted Actions or Skills			
Action or skill	*Almost always*	*Occasionally*	*Not yet*
1.			
2.			
3.			
4.			
5.			

Matrix

Subjects	Attributes					

A Web

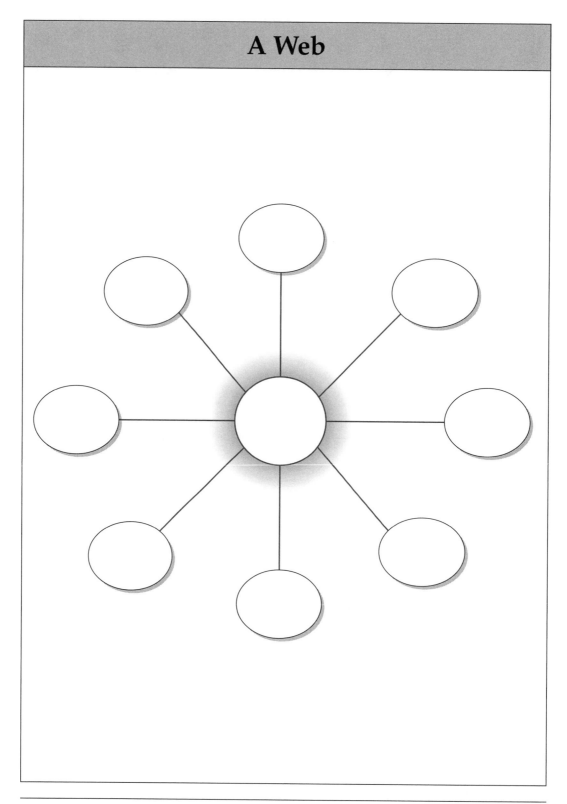

Element

Elements are pure substances that contain only one kind of atom. Two or more of these atoms may bond together to form molecules. Elements are the simplest substances known. Only about one hundred of them have been found in nature on earth. Elements cannot be chemically changed into other substances. Elements are homogeneous—all parts of an element look and act like all other parts of the same element. Some common elements are oxygen, hydrogen, copper, iron, gold, aluminum, and carbon.

Compound

Compounds are pure substances whose molecules are always identical. Atoms of two or more elements bond together to make molecules of compounds. Water molecules, for example, always contain two hydrogen atoms bonded to one oxygen atom. Silica molecules always contain one silicon atom bonded to two oxygen atoms. In a molecule of table salt, one sodium atom is bonded to one chlorine atom to produce sodium chloride. Compounds can be chemically broken apart into the elements that formed them. Compounds are homogeneous— all parts of a compound look and act like all other parts of the same compound. Millions of compounds are known. Some common compounds are salt, sugar, water, carbon dioxide, baking soda, and sulfuric acid.

Mixture

Mixtures contain two or more elements or compounds that are not chemically combined. The composition of a mixture may vary—there are lots of different ways to make salt water, for example. The percents of the two substances in the mixture will not always be the same. Mixtures may be separated physically or chemically. To separate a salt water mixture, you could just let the water evaporate out of the mixture. Mixtures are not always this easy to separate. It may be very tricky to separate a mixture of salt and sugar. Mixtures may be homogeneous—all parts of the mixture may look and act the same. Milk and mayonnaise are homogeneous mixtures. Mixtures may also be heterogeneous—different parts of the mixture may look and act differently. Asphalt and wood are heterogeneous mixtures. Millions of mixtures are known. There are more natural mixtures than elements or compounds. Some common mixtures are milk, wood, vinegar, concrete, brick, dirt, dishwater, and a pail of garbage.

Storyboard

Clint Cody is a modern-day cattle rancher in southern Wyoming. He runs his cattle on several thousand acres of grassland and forest. Clint loves ranching, except for one problem. It is really hard dealing with issues caused by several kinds of dinosaurs. You see, dinosaurs never became extinct. Clint must deal with dinosaur-related situations each day. Draw a storyboard that shows one day in Clint's life.

Right-Angle Thinking

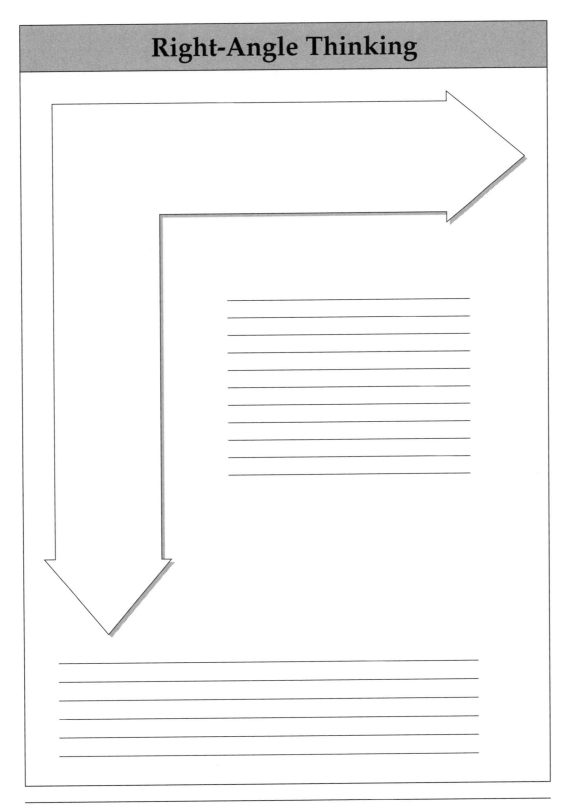

Lesson Planning Guide

Lesson Title:

Background:

Standards:

Focus Activity:

Objective:

Input:

Activity:

Cognitive Discussion:

Metacognitive Discussion:

Closure and Assessment:

NOTES

References and Recommended Readings

American Chemical Society. (2006). *ChemCom: Chemistry in the community* (5th ed.). New York: W. H. Freeman.

American Federation of Teachers. (2002). *Teaching English-language learners: What does the research say?* Retrieved February 7, 2008, from http://www.aft.org/pubs-reports/downloads/teachers/policy14.pdf

Andrade, A. (1999). *Ways of teaching thinking.* Retrieved February 14, 2008, from http://learnweb.harvard.edu/alps/thinking/ways.cfm

Aronson, E. (1978). *The jigsaw classroom.* Beverly Hills, CA: Sage Publications.

Beckett, E., & Haley, P. (2000). Using standards to integrate academic language into ESL fluency. *The Clearing House, 74*(2), 102–104.

Bellanca, J. (2007). *A guide to graphic organizers, second edition.* Thousand Oaks, CA: Corwin Press.

Bellanca, J. (1990). *Keep them thinking: Level III.* Palatine, IL: IRI/Skylight Publishing, Inc.

Bellanca, J., & Fogarty, R. (1986). *Catch them thinking: A handbook of classroom strategies.* Thousand Oaks, CA: Corwin Press.

Bellanca, J., & Fogarty, R. (2001). *Blueprints for achievement in the cooperative classroom.* Palatine, IL: IRI/Skylight Publishing, Inc.

Berman, S. (2008). *Performance-based learning, second edition.* Thousand Oaks, CA: Corwin Press.

Boothe, D. (2000). Looking beyond the ESL label. *Principal Leadership, 1*(4), 30–35.

Brilliant, C. D. G. (2001). *Parental involvement in education: Attitudes and activities of Spanish-speakers affected by training.* Retrieved February 14, 2008, from http://brj.asu.edu/v253/pdf/ar2.pdf

Brinkerhoff, R. F. (1992). *One minute readings: Issues in science, technology and society.* Menlo Park, CA: The Alternative Publishing Group (Addison Wesley).

Buzan, T. (2002). *How to mind map.* New York: HarperCollins.

Caine, R. N., Caine, G., McClintic, C., & Klimek, K. (2005). *12 brain-mind learning principles in action: The fieldbook for making connections, teaching, and the human brain.* Thousand Oaks, CA: Corwin Press.

Christensen, J. (1991). *Global science: Energy, resources, environment.* Dubuque, IA: Kendall/Hunt Publishing Company.

Cognitive Skills Group, Harvard Project Zero. (1998). *Introducing the thinking classroom.* Retrieved August 17, 2007, from http://learnweb.harvard.edu/alps/thinking/

Collins, G. (2001). *Mediated and collaborative learning for students with learning disabilities: "This is about life, it's about the rules of life."* A dissertation presented for the Doctor of Education Degree, The University of Tennessee, Knoxville.

Cotton, K. (1991). *Teaching thinking skills.* Retrieved August 7, 2007, from http://www.nwrel.org/scpd/sirs/6/cu11.html

Cronin Jones, L. (2003). Are lectures a thing of the past? *Journal of College Science Teaching, 23*(7), 453–457.

Crowe, M. (2001). *Investigating the ways of nature: An in-class experiment.* Retrieved October 3, 2007, from http://www.hssonline.org/teach_res/CoE/activities/nature

de Bono, E. (1973). *Lateral thinking: Creativity step by step.* New York: Harper Paperbacks.

Egbert, J., & Simich-Dudgeon, C. (2001). Providing support for non-native learners of English in the social studies classroom. *The Social Studies, 92*(1), 22–25.

Ellis, E. (2004). *Q & A: What's the big deal with graphic organizers?* Retrieved September 25, 2007, from http://www.graphicorganizers.com/Sara/ArticlesAbout/Q&A%20Graphic%20Organizers.pdf

Feuerstein, R. (1980). *Instrumental enrichment: An intervention program for cognitive modifiability.* Baltimore, MD: University Park Press.

Fogarty, R., & Bellanca, J. (1987). *Patterns for thinking: Patterns for transfer.* Palatine, IL: IRI/Skylight Publishing, Inc.

Fogarty, R., & Haack, J. (1986). *The thinking log.* Palatine, IL: IRI/Skylight Publishing, Inc.

Fogarty, R., & Opeka, K. (1988). *Start them thinking: A handbook of classroom strategies for the early years.* Palatine, IL: IRI/Skylight Publishing, Inc.

Galyam, N., & LeGrange, L. (2003). Teaching thinking skills to learners with special needs. *International Journal of Special Education, 18*(2), 84–94.

Gotimer, K. K. (Ed.). (1993). *Science, technology, and society* (text series). Columbus, OH: Globe Book Co., Simon & Schuster.

Graphic.org. (n.d.). *Brainstorming web.* Retrieved October 3, 2007, from http://www.graphic.org/goindex.html

Greenberg, K. (1996). *Learning how to learn.* Retrieved February 14, 2008, from http://www.context.org/ICLIB/IC27/Greenbrg.htm

Gridley, C., & Roberts, R. (1992). *Asking better classroom questions.* Portland, ME: J. Weston Walch.

Halter, J. (n.d.). *Metacognition.* Retrieved October 28, 2007, from http://coe.sdsu.edu/eet/Articles/metacognition/start.htm

Hassard, J. (2004). *The art of teaching science.* New York: Oxford University Press.

Holmes, O. W. (1916). *The poet at the breakfast table.* Boston, MA: Houghton Mifflin.

Jenkins, D. C. (1991). *Amusing problems in physics.* Portland, ME: J. Weston Walch.

Johnson, D. W., Johnson, R., & Holubec, E. (1988). *Advanced cooperative learning.* Edina, MN: Interaction Book Company.

Johnson, D. W., Johnson, R., & Holubec, E. (1988). *Cooperation in the classroom* (revised edition). Edina, MN: Interaction Book Company.

Johnson, D. W., Johnson, R., & Holubec, E. (1987). *Structuring cooperative learning: The 1987 handbook of lesson plans for teachers.* Edina, MN: Interaction Book Company.

Johnson, D. W., Johnson, R., & Holubec, E. (1986). *Circles of learning: Cooperation in the classroom* (revised edition). Edina, MN: Interaction Book Company.

Kluger, J. (2007). The power of birth order. *Time, 170*(18), 42–48.

Learning Point Associates. (1995). *Metacognition.* Retrieved February 4, 2008, from http://www.ncrel.org/sdrs/areas/issues/students/learning/lr1metn.htm

METIRI Group. (2003). *Twenty-first century skills*. Retrieved August 17, 2007, from http://www.metiri.com/21st%20Century%20Skills/PDFtwentyfirst%20century%20skills.pdf

Meyer, L. (2000). Barriers to meaningful instruction for English learners. *Theory Into Practice, 39*(4), 228–236.

National Academies Press. (1995). *National science education standards*. Retrieved August 7, 2007, from http://www.nap.edu/readingroom/books/nses/html

National Science Teachers Association. (2007). *The integral role of laboratory investigations in science instruction*. Retrieved August 17, 2007, from http://www.nsta.org/about/positions/laboratory.aspx

Northwest Regional Educational Laboratory. (2007). *Is there only one way to do science inquiry?* Retrieved September 25, 2007, from http://www.nwrel.org/msec/science_inq/answers.html

Ogle, D. (1986). K-W-L: A teaching model that develops active reading of expository text. *The Reading Teacher, 37*(6), 564–570.

Pellino, K. (2007). *Effective strategies for teaching English language learners*. Retrieved September 25, 2007, from http://www.teach-nology.com/tutorials/teaching/esl/

Perkins, D. (2003). *Making thinking visible*. Retrieved August 17, 2007, from http://www.newhorizons.org/strategies/thinking/perkins.htm

SCANS. (1991). *What work requires of schools*. Retrieved February 15, 2008, from the U.S. Department of Labor Web site http://wdr.doleta.gov/SCANS/whatwork/

Sylwester, R. (1995). *A celebration of neurons: An educator's guide to the human brain*. Alexandria, VA: Association for Supervision and Curriculum Development.

Weiss, C. (1993). *But how do we get them to think?* Retrieved August 7, 2007, from http://orpheum.ctl.mnscu.edu/teach/resources/pod/Packet3/buthowdowegetthemtothink

Winkler, A., Bernstein, L., Schachter, M., & Wolfe, S. (1989). *Concepts and challenges in science*. Columbus, OH: Globe Book Co., Simon & Schuster.

Index